LOST GODDESSES

LOST GODDESSES
A Kaleidoscope on Porn

Giorgio Tricarico

KARNAC

First published in 2018 by
Karnac Books Ltd
118 Finchley Road
London NW3 5HT

Copyright © 2018 to Giorgio Tricarico

The right of Giorgio Tricarico to be identified as the author of this work has been asserted in accordance with §§ 77 and 78 of the Copyright Design and Patents Act 1988.

All rights reserved. No part of this publication may be reproduced, stored in a retrieval system, or transmitted, in any form or by any means, electronic, mechanical, photocopying, recording, or otherwise, without the prior written permission of the publisher.

British Library Cataloguing in Publication Data

A C.I.P. for this book is available from the British Library

ISBN-13: 978-1-78220-532-6

Typeset by V Publishing Solutions Pvt Ltd., Chennai, India

www.karnacbooks.com

CONTENTS

ACKNOWLEDGEMENTS   vii

ABOUT THE AUTHOR   viii

INTRODUCTION   ix

CHAPTER ONE
Porn and technology   1

CHAPTER TWO
Porn and phantoms   7

CHAPTER THREE
Porn and seduction   13

CHAPTER FOUR
Porn and the roses of Kenya   19

CHAPTER FIVE
Porn and no limit   25

CHAPTER SIX
Porn and shadow   33

CHAPTER SEVEN
Porn and as if   45

CHAPTER EIGHT
Porn and divinity   53

CHAPTER NINE
Porn and lost goddesses   67

NOTES   79

REFERENCES   91

APPENDIX
The quest for meaning after the end of meaning   95

INDEX   109

ACKNOWLEDGEMENTS

I dedicate this work to Kata-Riina Heinonen-Tricarico, whose loveful encouragement has been fundamental, and to Joonas and Nooa, who gave birth to me as a father.

I am deeply grateful to Nina Kanevskaya, and Arlene Landau for their careful reading of my manuscript during its drafting, for their support, and their valuable comments and reflections on the topic of this work.

I am deeply grateful to Alyson Silverwood, for her outstanding job of copyediting and sharpening my English, and to Cecily Blench, Constance Govindin, Kate Pearce, Oliver Rathbone, and Rod Tweedy at Karnac Books.

Since writing a book requires, among many other things, nourishment for the soul, I am deeply grateful to Jeff Buckley's *You and I* album, to P. J. Harvey's *The Hope Six Demolition Project*, to Radiohead's *A Moon Shaped Pool*, and to Savages' *Adore Life*. Their music has been a very precious presence during the whole process of letting ideas flow and writing them down.

This work is my offering to all the unwitting goddesses I have seen during my life.

ABOUT THE AUTHOR

Giorgio Tricarico is a clinical psychologist, a Jungian analyst, a member of the International Association for Analytical Psychology, and the first President of the Finnish-Estonian Group for Analytical Psychology. He has worked with adult patients since 1998, and has given several lectures and seminars on relevant issues in analytical psychology. Since 2009, he has been living and working in Helsinki, Finland, as a psychologist, psychotherapist, a Jungian analyst and a supervisor. He is the author of *The Labyrinth of Possibility: A Therapeutic Factor in Analytical Practice*, and has written a number of essays and short stories. He is also a singer, a guitarist, and a songwriter.

INTRODUCTION

In one of the main Italian daily newspapers, a coloured map illustrates the field in which many books about porn find their place. On the left side of the map, we see the pictures of the "pro-sex" authors, together with the titles of their works, while on the right, those dubbed as "anti-porn". Only two authors are set in the middle, under the label of "problematic".[1]

Despite the fact that the article aimed to offer a panoramic view of the publications on the subject up to then, it is interesting to notice how porn evokes immediately a pro/versus polarisation. The opinions are *divided*, as the subtitle of the article points out.

Many authors strongly underline how porn abases women's dignity, showing the die-hard male domination of women to the highest degrees; while others emphasise porn's subversive role against the dominant values and aesthetics of our time.

A polarised, emotional position is rarely a good starting point to comprehend a complex phenomenon, as porn is. *Complectere*, to embrace, to keep between one's own arms, is the Latin root of the adjective *complex*. Porn is definitely a complex object. In the attempt to comprehend it, we should be able to embrace, to hold between our arms, several different elements and opposites—tolerating their contradictions, even.

Sym-balleín, to throw together, is the ancient Greek root of the word *symbol*. Porn is definitely a symbol, as C. G. Jung intended it: a place where several elements are thrown together, referring, alluding, aiming to express something partially unutterable.

Porn is a complex symbol of our times, emerging in a specific moment of the history of human consciousness. Porn is a symbol and a complex object, immediately able to evoke the strongest polarised reactions, as it is dealing with one of the most powerful psychic elements, that is, sexuality. If our aim is to comprehend it, we should try to go beyond polarisations, beyond ranting and praise.

Internet porn is the main topic of this work. In the last two decades, it has become one of the biggest businesses in the world, with a myriad of websites dealing with it. Accordingly, publications and books have grown in number, illuminating different aspects of internet porn's complexity. Some sociologists have considered the historical evolution of mass porn, and its impact on the lives of men and women and on their relationships in the contemporary world; some philosophers have explored the nuances of what they consider to be the core elements, especially from the point of view of deconstructivism and Lacanian theory; finally, some clinicians and psychotherapists have dealt with the forms of addiction related to internet porn, and with the dangers of a prolonged exposure to porn imagery.

This work aims to explore some aspects of internet porn from the perspective of analytical psychology, confronting it as a symbol of the complexity of the human psyche, emerged in a specific moment of the history of consciousness.

The emotionally polarised readers will surely find in the following chapters several elements to strengthen their contempt for porn, and their "against" attitude; but at the same time, they will be compelled to extend their critical attitude to a much wider degree, as porn is just one particularly evident and unsettling symbol of our current way-of-being-in-the-world.

Those who feel a fascination for porn imagery, openly declared or hard to confess, perhaps coloured with guilt and shame, may understand its deepest resonances with psychic contents that need to find a place in our world, in ways still to be experienced and embodied.

Pórne, in ancient Greek, meant the lowest-level "prostitute", as could be found in brothels, taverns, and public streets. The root of the word appears to be connected with *pernémi*, "to sell, to trade". The *pórnai*, the prostitutes, were selling themselves and their bodies, in the most hideous conditions of wretchedness.

As Nancy Qualls-Corbett points out, in the archaic and in the classical eras in Greece, "they were subject to abuse, arrest and banishment from the city, not allowed to mix with society and not allowed on the streets in the daytime. It was forbidden for them to enter the temples or to participate in any religious ceremony" (Qualls-Corbett, 1988, p. 38); "The degradation of the profane prostitute, who represents the dark side of feminine sexuality, was profound" (p. 39).

Filthy, unclean, exposed, the profane prostitute was considered a mere instrument, needed and essential albeit despised, just like a slave. A body with no name, sold and offered with no appreciation for her individuality. Dirty flesh, to be used, abused, and degraded.

Nestled in the word "porn", we still find the meaning of making money out of one's own body and sexual activity, the idea of degrading, and the patriarchal hypocrisy of disdain of something actually needed and desired.

This work deals with the phenomenon of porn, as made possible by the development of technology during the last hundred and fifty years, and particularly with *mass porn*, whose birth could be set in 1969, when the Danish Code of Laws allowed the production and the distribution of hard-core pictures and movies. A further symbolic date for the birth of porn as a mass phenomenon was perhaps June 1972, when *Deep Throat* was projected for the first time in a movie theatre in New York.

The reflections in this book will mainly consider porn intended as images to arouse sexual excitement in heterosexual men. I will exclude gay porn, as I believe I would be less able to see some phenomena from the perspective of a gay person, albeit many of the issues I will explore surely also apply to porn intended for gay people. I will exclude BDSM[2] porn as well, in as much as its inner logic is very specific, dealing with power, humiliation, administration of pain and pleasure, negotiating and controlling all these dimensions within an agreed frame.

I use the word *porn*, and not *pornography*, although in publications on this topic they are often regarded as synonyms. As I deeply value etymology and the rich imaginal activity that it allows, I cannot disregard the evidence that *pornography* refers exactly to written material (*graphein*, in ancient Greek, "to write, to draw") about *pórnai*, prostitutes. The word *pornography* had been aptly used for literary productions published from the eighteenth century onwards.[3] I reckon that to extend its meaning to pictures or movies showing sexual acts is basically incorrect. Whereas contemporary dictionaries endorse this shift in meaning, I prefer to stick to etymology.

This book is addressed not only to psychotherapists, but to anyone who is interested in understanding porn as a phenomenon of the society of technology, its inner logic, and its multiple layers and connections.

The language used to speak about porn needs to share its codes, its slang, its rawness and directness; I reckon it's unlikely that the reader who might be offended, disgusted, or shocked by this kind of explicit language would choose to read such a collection of essays on porn. Nevertheless, I will try to use notes as the main place where the most unsettling elements will be described in detail.

Each chapter will focus on one single element—one colour, so to say—leading the whole book to become a kind of kaleidoscope. It is in the combination of all these colours that the object "mass porn" might be captured in some of its complexity, and the resulting photograph may change, according to the rotation of the kaleidoscope the reader may choose.

Porn Papers

CHAPTER ONE

Porn and technology

A common anecdote narrates that five minutes after photography had been invented, in 1826, a woman was posing naked in front of the photographic lens. The same is said to have happened some decades later, when cinematography came to light. It might sound pretty trivial to underline it, but porn owes its very existence to the development of technological devices.

Camerae obscurae, daguerreotypes, monochrome and colour photography, together with the invention of the motion picture, made sexually explicit pictures and short movies possible by the end of the nineteenth century.[1]

The chance to get hold of such materials, however, was pretty scarce for the largest part of the population of Western countries, this novelty being available only for minorities and elites for several decades.[2] From the 1950s onwards, though, eight-millimetre films and cine-cameras gave impetus to a growing production of erotic movies, shot in black and white, but these largely remained outside the mainstream movie industry until the 1960s. It was during this decade that sexually explicit material started circulating more and more, in the form of magazines and movies, in an interesting parallel with other significant social changes. In fact, this rapidly growing phenomenon mingled with the subversion of bourgeois morality and values, the feminist struggle for equality, and the separation of sexuality from the reproductive function.

The production of black-and-white porn movies flourished in Soho, London, from the beginning of the 1960s, and was to find a more permissive environment of potential consumers in Denmark, which subsequently became a leading producer of porn material, together with Sweden.

As previously mentioned, in 1969 Denmark was the first country to legally allow the production and the distribution of hard-core movies and pictures, followed by the United States in 1970. Mass porn could be considered to have been born with these legal acts, as from that moment on, it was more and more possible for everyone to get in touch with porn material, buying magazines in some newspaper kiosks and watching movies in the new-born porn-movie theatres.

The next technological step was going to be the invention of VCR (Video Cassette Recording) systems, which started in the middle of the 1970s, to reach their boom in the early 1980s. Actually, VCR systems became popular and widespread precisely due to hard-core VHS videotape sales.

Dominating the Western market until the mid-1990s, a VHS tape made it very simple to view porn at home, avoiding the difficulties and possibly the social shame of physically going to public places like movie theatres. Renting or buying porn videotapes became more and more handy, while VHS functions such as forward, rewind, and slow motion changed the approachability of porn movies. Thanks to these functions, it was possible to skip all the unnecessary acting in order to reach directly the favourite sex scenes, and to go back to them any time one felt like it.

DVDs substituted VCR technology during the 1990s, but the accessibility of porn material did not change significantly, until the World Wide Web took over. Although it is still possible to buy porn DVDs and magazines, the internet enables the viewing of porn material online, just by connecting computers, tablets, and mobile phones to one of the thousands of free porn websites, such as xvideos, pornhub, or youporn.

In fewer than forty years, therefore, we have witnessed a tremendous increase in the reachability of porn material, together with its progressive dematerialisation, from paper magazines to videotapes, from DVDs to video files. This dematerialisation has gone hand in hand with the decreasing need to physically go and look for porn materials; walking gingerly to a newspaper kiosk, a sex shop, or a movie theatre was gradually replaced by the discreet purchase of DVDs online, subscription to a pay-per-view TV channel, and eventually to accessing porn files in streaming for free, safely sitting on one's own couch with a tablet or a laptop. Furthermore, the web evolution has made it possible for people to become active users, and not only passive consumers, as it is nowadays quite simple for basically everyone to shoot porn pictures or videos and upload them in video file format online.

This short survey of the different phases in the production, the distribution, and the accessibility of porn material aims to underline how porn and technology have been deeply entwined with each other since the very start. Hence, porn must be considered a technological product. This product is currently codified in immaterial files, infinitely duplicable, reproducible, and so subject to the logic of several other products developed in our technological society.

Speaking of technology, it would be remiss to prescind from the critical work of the German philosopher Günther Anders.[3] After a deplorable delay of thirty-five years, a first English translation of the second volume of his main work has finally appeared on the web, together with some extracts from the first volume, the publication of which dated back to 1956.[4] Reversal of perspective is the peculiar way to proceed with Anders' "philosophical anthropology in the epoch of technocracy", as he himself defines it. This reversal first of all implies that it's no more possible to ask ourselves what we can do with technology, rather we should ask what technology can do with (or to) us. Anders maintains that:

> the world in which we live and which surrounds us is a technological world, to such an extent that we are no longer permitted to say that, in our historical situation, technology is just one thing that exists among us like other things, but that instead we must say that now, history unfolds in the situation of the world known as world of technology, and therefore technology has actually become the subject of history, alongside of which we are merely co-historical.
>
> (Anders, 2007b, p. 3)

Technology is the current subject of history, the *zeitgeist* of our time, and our fate.

The system of apparatuses is *our world* and we, as individuals, are undergoing transformations in our psychic, emotional, and ethical way-of-being, still to be focused on and explored.

If we define the second industrial revolution as the period during which machines started being produced by way of other machines, its outcome is a world where the production of products corresponds to the production of means of productions, that in turn produce other means of productions, and so on, until final products are created.

These last are no more means of production but means of consumption. Their consumption produces the situation in which the production by way of machines is required and necessary.

Our role is hence to use and consume products *so that* the production can continue. Products have a hunger to be consumed, so to say, and in order to fulfil this hunger, we need to have a need for them.

But since this need does not necessarily arise naturally in us, it has to be produced as well. The third industrial revolution implies the *production of needs in us*, by way of a specific industry, that is, advertisement or, more elegantly, marketing, and by way of the products themselves, in as much as they are capable of inducing the need in us by way of their use and consumption, and by way of programmed obsolescence, so that the production will not stop. In the meantime, the technological apparatus as a whole keeps growing, in terms of potential to infinitely expand and to reach goals, following the commandment "Everything that can be done, must be done". One barely visible result is that we all are transformed in some sense into unpaid employees of the technological apparatus, so that it continues to expand itself and to function, that is, to produce.[5]

These are some of the coordinates of the epoch of the third industrial revolution, according to Anders' view. In such a world, technological inventions are never just technological inventions,[6] because

> every machine, once it exists, already *constitutes* a way of its utilisation by the mere fact of its functioning [...] We are always molded by every apparatus, regardless of the purpose for which we think of using it or imagine it being used for [...] since it always presupposes or estabilishes a determined relation between us and our kind, between us and things, between things and us.
>
> (Anders, 2007b, p. 200)

The idea that technological inventions are just neutral tools, and all that matters is how we use them, is dismissed as a naivety to be openly fought, a mere illusion, probably aimed to preserve our faded freedom from the system of apparatuses that we have built and currently inhabit.

Having something compels one not only to use it, but to need it: in the end, one does not have what is useful, but what is imposed.

The example of Coca-Cola, given by Anders, could clarify the insidious inversion implicit in our common use of technological products. Thirst is definitely a basic need, but we cannot say that *thirst for Coca-Cola* is. The tendency of thirst to be directed towards Coca-Cola and not to water is due to the fact that the effect of Coca-Cola is exactly to stimulate thirst, precisely a thirst for Coca-Cola.

The need is essentially produced by the product itself, together with the massive influence of advertisement and marketing. The need produced by the product ensures the increase of the production of the product, via our cooperation as consumers/employees.

The need to be permanently connected is a flawless example of the same principle, updated to our current times. Surely we cannot say that being permanently connected is a basic need, like hunger, thirst, or sexuality. Still, the evidence of thousands of people, bowing to the screens of their mobiles and tablets in trains, in metros, in bars, or walking on the street, should suggest that the need to be permanently connected has been absorbed by the majority of us.

The production of more powerful devices, of their accessories, of thousands of constantly implementing apps, have the biggest supporters precisely among the users, *bona fide* convinced that they are only using tools that expand their own freedom to express themselves, and that make their own lives more comfortable or entertaining.

As Anders aptly summarises,

> a considerable part of today's commodities are not actually there for us; instead, we are ourselves, as buyers and consumers, those who are there to assure their further production. Thus, if our need to consume (and, as a result, our lifestyle) has been created—or at least marked—so that commodities can be sold, we are only *means*, and, as such, we are ontologically subject to the ends.[7]

Mass porn is just one of the myriad of technological objects, products, and services that form our modern world. As such, porn is subject to the same dynamics as any other product, including a possible addictive quality that compels consumers to spend more and more time surfing on porn websites, looking for the ultimate fragment of an unfulfillable desire.

The English word *addiction* comes from Latin *addictus*, which meant "delivered as a slave to someone". The common expression used in Italian is *dipendenza*, which condensates in one word "addiction, dependence, dependency, reliance". As human beings, we definitely depend on our technological world in manifold ways: our physical sustenance, our health care, our learning and socialisation processes, and ultimately our survival currently rely, to some extent, or even totally, on the "system of apparatuses", as Anders calls it.

Moreover, our current *mater*-ialistic society embodies the *mater*-nal function, that of a mother (indeed *mater* in Latin), in a distorted way, as it transforms us into dependent, permanent children, by nourishing our needs, creating new ones, and fulfilling them, but never enough, in order to perpetuate itself.

From dependency to addiction is not a very long step. Allegedly, it's just a matter of degree on a *continuum*. At any rate, the technological apparatus tends towards addictions, as they represent the absolute state that would ensure its expansion and its duration.[8]

There is no doubt that more and more people are running serious risk of developing an addiction (in the etymological sense, as we mentioned, of being slave) to porn images, compelling them to spend an increasing amount of their time surfing on the net, and manifesting in withdrawal symptoms. Presumably, researchers would find very similar results were they to explore the use and the common abuse of smart phones, of social networks, of video games, of websites, and so on.

Dependency/addiction is *de facto* the current condition in which we are immersed, and where this is not yet so, it is subtly cultivated, encouraged, and even praised.

Although we may reasonably make every effort to get rid of the most severe forms of addiction, including that to porn, this seems to me like trying to turn off an electric fan in the middle of a windstorm. As a matter of fact, there has never been in the whole of human history such a deployment of forces and means aimed at teaching us to need, to depend on, and to be addicted to what is offered, in every area of our lives.

CHAPTER TWO

Porn and phantoms

Whether in static or moving pictures, porn always presents a defiant, provocative image. Seductive, repulsive, fascinating, appalling—a porn image instantly arouses a powerful emotional response in the viewer, no matter whether the feeling-tone is on the side of pleasure or on that of disgust.

Following again Günther Anders' reflections, let's focus on another unmistakable aspect of our contemporary reality: more and more, we do not participate directly in the world, we rather consume its image. The German philosopher dubbed "iconomania" the systematic overflow of images characteristic of the era of the third industrial revolution. We are supplied with the world mostly through its images, pre-pared (literally "previously arranged") for us.

Anders defines these prepared images of the world as *phantoms*, in the sense of half-present and half-absent, so to say, real and apparent, at the same time. When we see an image, what is portrayed is absent, it is not physically in front of us, but it is concurrently present *in effigie*. As images of the world, phantoms possess a bi-dimensional ubiquitous nature, and can be reproduced virtually innumerable times, just like any other assembly-line product.

The first visible consequence of the world coming to us as phantom is that we are no more compelled to go to the world, in order to explore or experience it. The world is presented to us in such a manner that it seems to exist *for us*, and is consumed *as if* we were experiencing it. Accordingly, we can say we are no more *in* the world, but only consumers of it: whichever event is shown, we do not actually participate in it, rather we consume its image, or phantom.

Anders wrote these astounding reflections in reference to television and radio broadcast, decades before the birth of the World Wide Web. His essay entitled "The obsolescence of privacy" was in fact written in 1958. There we can read lines like

> the events of the world are delivered to your home by way of radio and television; they are supplied just like gas or water [...] the outside world [...] is no longer presented to us as world [...] it's not just an image of the world, either. Rather, it is presented as a *tertium*, as something *sui generis*, as a *phantom of the world*.
>
> (Anders, 2007b, p. 193)

Accordingly, each of us, as a mass media spectator, is transformed into a *cannibal of phantoms*, as Anders puts it. Able to access phantoms at any time we want, we can connect to and disconnect from them, in an illusory state of omnipotence, but inevitably, we are turned into mere eavesdroppers and voyeurs.

Already valid during the pioneering era of the first radio and TV broadcasting, these reflections flawlessly befit the epoch of internet and of digital, virtual realities. The world has been literally transferred into its image, and it has become possible to explore it sitting in one's own living room, on Google Maps, for instance.

Images of the world are daily supplied to everyone holding an internet connection, to the point that when something terrible happens, like a terrorist attack or an outbreak of war, it's easier to understand (literally, to get a picture of) what is going on for someone far away who follows the event via web, than for those actually involved in the real event.

Accordingly, voyeurism is the basic attitude evoked by these media—required by them, one might say—and this is valid not only for TV or web pages: social networks like Instagram or Facebook, namely those virtual places where what is private becomes public and what is public is potentially deliverable to any private individual, have the power to transform any user (read, consumer) into a voyeur as well.

Anders added that

> when the event is no longer attached to a specific location and can be reproduced virtually a number of times, it acquires the characteristics of an assembly-line product; and when we pay for having it delivered to our homes, it is a commodity [...] The metamorphosis of the world into something that is at my disposal has technically taken place.[1]

Since the world is basically brought to us as a commodity, and it's mostly accessible in its bi-dimensional images/phantoms, with just a click, its real, physical experience becomes superfluous. Being a voyeur is enough to give us the idea that we have experienced the reality.

All these reflections are extremely germane to our topic, since porn is *ab initio* a defiant, unsettling, fascinating image, entwined as it is with the invention and the development of visual reproduction devices, as previously explored.

Now that pictures and videos are codified into bits of information, porn has reached the state of immaterial and infinitely reproducible images, forming an immense erotic digitalised landscape, dubbed a *pornscape*. Among millions of other images on the web, porn pictures embody the perfect means of transformation of the user into a voyeur.

This result is not at all incidental, but it is precisely pursued: the sex scene, performed in reality elsewhere, is transformed into an image (a phantom, in Anders' terms), and eventually offered to the spectator's view in another space and time. The spectator is dragged into the porn scene precisely as a voyeur (spectator, from Latin *spectare*, "to watch", means only "he/she who watches"), the porn scene being a phantom of a real scene that has already happened in some past time.

The porn actresses' glance is turned to the camera eye, right into the eyes of the physically absent spectator (in turn, a phantom for the performers, when the scene was shot), inviting him to join her, hinting "I would do this *to you*, were you here". Porn apparently exists only *for us*.

There would be no porn, no need to record and reproduce sexually explicit images, without having the spectator in mind, as the final recipient. Our transformation into eavesdroppers and voyeurs is blatantly open, not at all hidden, as hinted by the common use of these terms in the past eras. In relation to porn, we are meant to be eavesdroppers and voyeurs: the porn scene is a show, and as such yearns to be shown to someone, in those precise roles.

The transformation of the user into a voyeur/spectator emphasises vision, as sight is obviously the dominant sense: while engaging with porn material, sight is on the sensory pedestal, and crouched at its base lies hearing, in the case of videos. Interestingly enough, the other three left-out senses, touch, smell, and taste, are phylogenetically the most archaic, and the predominant ones in real sex. The experience of touching the skin of a partner, its silkiness, its variations, its temperature, its sounds when caressed, the experience of tasting and smelling a partner's body, in all its nuances and unexpectedness, are necessarily excluded and precluded while watching porn.

The user is *reduced* to a voyeur, carrying the meaning of the reduction of the whole sensorial experience to one, maximum two, of the five senses. In fact, we cannot be *in touch* with porn material, but only connect to it by consuming its visual image.

In parallel with this reduction of the sensorial experience, we witness a transformation of the eye into a sex organ. The eroticised eye virtually penetrates every orifice,[2] situated as it is in places often unreachable by sight during real intercourse. Identified with the camera eye, our eye is present as a phantom on the porn scene, and can be seen as the *punkt* where the past time of the scene touches the present of our consumption of it.

Besides, the idea of the eye as a sex organ corresponds with the results of many neuroscientific researches about the predominance of vision in male sexual excitement, accounting for the immediate and almost unavoidable attraction to porn images by the majority of men.

Porn material is commonly divided into brands. Every website appears to be a dictionary of genres, a catalogue of desires, a sort of virtual supermarket, where rows and rows of shelves display carefully what the spectator might like (and what he will learn to like). Vision is the main sense not only while watching a porn scene, a clip, a video, or an image, but is right from the start the means to surf the catalogue, to explore the shelves. Moreover, the presence of a pre-view function, a sort of expansion of vision in time, enables the viewer to fore-see, to see in advance, what will happen in the clip.

Inadvertently, a big part of the sexual excitement, if not the the biggest, becomes the adrenalinic phase of the search and pre-view, even more than masturbating to the chosen scene. Those extremely rare male patients who have been willing to tell me some details about their use of porn during our analytical sessions reported *the search* for the right scene or the right woman as the most thrilling part of the whole experience of internet porn. Some of them also became aware that, together with this excitement and thrill, an unsettling sensation was to be felt in the background: a subtle push to go on looking, as the best image may be the next one, just round the corner, so to say. The modern sirens do not really sing, rather they keep repeating to an earplugs-less Ulysses "Go on! Keep on searching! The best is always the next."

Acknowledging this unsettling sensation is to gain awareness that *customer dissatisfaction* is always one of the main goals of any product or service in our current world. A satisfied client, in fact, is the most horrific outcome, as they would probably not buy another product or service soon enough. Dissatisfaction is the real goal, and it is implicitly pursued, despite what is blatantly declared, as it guarantees the production will never stop, in porn as well as in any other area.

Our reality is constantly awash with images/phantoms, porn being just a part of this flood, and accordingly we are turned into voyeurs and cannibalic consumers of those very images. Image is the way par excellence the world is offered to us, may it be as an image of a commodity (a product, a trip, a place, a service, and so on) or may the image itself be a commodity, as in porn, and "offers are today's commandments", as Anders maintains. The aim of these commandments is to teach us what to need, what to desire, and how to desire it, even.

As mentioned in Chapter One, inverting what we commonly believe, the aim of the offer is exactly to produce a demand.[3] In this respect, porn is no exception; on the contrary.

Expanding our reflections beyond the topic of this work, the offer of commodities through images/phantoms, in order to teach us what we should need and how, could be seen as a part of that *manufacturing consent* aptly described by Noam Chomsky and Edward S. Herman.[4]

What is important is to reflect on how our daily relationship with all sorts of bi-dimensional phantoms is possibly affecting and changing our psyche, our emotions, our ethical attitude towards what is represented, and ultimately our way-of-being-in-the-world. The habit of dealing with images, our transformation into voyeurs, the loss of a complex sensorial experience to the sole advantage of sight and hearing, the resultant estrangement from the actual world, the unprecedented need to be permanently connected and to have an online identity, the emotional distancing, and the potential for addiction to all this, in no way appertains only to frequent porn users.

All these phenomena were brought to my attention a few days ago, when I was crossing a bridge on the River Vantaa, in Helsinki, not far from where I live. An older lady, a teenager, and a little girl, in single file, were crossing the same bridge in the opposite direction, a few metres between them, their heads bowed over their mobile phones. They were together, walking slightly clumsily, with just some peripheric attention not to bang into someone, oblivious of (or indifferent to) the painful beauty of the landscape-painting they were actually a part of: the dark green river flowing silently under the bridge, the blossoming forest on its banks, after the long bare Finnish winter, the blaze of the darkening sky, littered with pink cotton clouds. They crossed the painting, unabashed. They were inhabiting a different world, at least in that moment, a world of images calling to them, absent but present, and strong enough to subtract them from the world I lived in.

CHAPTER THREE

Porn and seduction

Walking out of a café one day, my at that time six-year-old son's glance was enraptured by the big black pair of eyes of a plush toy, holding a guitar in his little paws. Of course, my son asked to be bought the pet, only to receive a resolute "no" from his father, deterred by the ludicrous price of the toy. During the evening, at home, my son sketched the very plush pet, emphasising its big eyes. On his way to bed, I caught a shadow of sadness in his countenance, and when I asked him what was going on, he burst out crying, and explained, with the most harrowing voice, that he kept thinking of the plush pet's eyes: he actually drew the pet with the painful awareness he would never seen it again. His tears were genuine and sincere, expressing a profound sorrow, a sort of nostalgia, for something that had not come about. Unarmed by his child's pain, I bought two of those plush pets the following day, one for him and one for his little brother; of course, in my heart, with the most thorough hatred for merchandising.

What has this anecdote to do with porn?

In her *Pornified: How Pornography Is Damaging Our Lives, Our Relationships, and Our Families*, an alarmed Pamela Paul expresses the idea that porn has infiltrated several aspects of our current world, to the extent that it may be denoted as "pornified". A contributor to *Time* magazine, Pamela Paul compiles a journalistic report on what she considers to be the growing influence of porn on American society, able to transform its culture and to corrupt the lives of the majority. She describes how porn has become integrated into American, and more broadly Western, culture, expressed, for example, by pop music stars in their videoclips, by fashion imagery and clothes production, appropriated by social network users, in the way they portray themselves in their profile pictures, and so on. A touch of porn is considered cool, nowadays, transgression being actually the norm. Paul's book is basically a clarion call against the pervasive porn colonisation of our world, and the presumed negative consequences on the lives, careers, relationships, marriages, and sexuality of porn viewers.

Porn materials in the internet are more and more accessed by children before puberty, and one can surely wonder about the negative effects of the exposure to contents that cannot yet be mentalised or embodied by a child. The impact on the processes of identity formation during teenage years, including development of sexual identity, of porn material that can be extreme, pretty unrealistic, and inclined to desensitise the viewer, is a matter of legitimate concern.

The presence and the help of adults, in the role of mediators between children, teenagers, and the manifold aspects of internet porn, could be extremely precious. But this would imply that those adults have comprehended the phenomenon at a deeper level, something that Paul's book, like the majority of books about porn, is not so much helping us to do.

The idea of porn as a colonising negative force that gradually but relentlessly infiltrates a previously moral and non-sexual society, to the extent that nowadays the world has become "pornified", for instance, is misleading and mystifying. In fact, porn has not at all been the *primum movens* of the sexualisation, or pornification, of our world.

As previously explored, the availability of commodities, products, and services has attained a scale that would have been unimaginable in previous eras. Capitalism and technology have been walking arm in arm for more than two centuries, and in the epoch of the third industrial revolution they conceived a scenario where not only products and services, but also needs, have to be produced, to ensure their self-perpetuation.

The industry assigned to the production of needs is advertisement. In his essay entitled "The obsolescence of the individual", Anders maintains that

> We do not live among things that surround us silently and indifferently. [...] From the moment when all the objects of all types have been infected by all the objects of the current dominant type, that is, of the commodity type, it is instead correct to say that *our world is*, in advance, *a universe of advertisement*. It consists in things that offer themselves to us and solicit us. *Advertising is a mode of existence of our world.*

In the ocean of commodities that surrounds us, Anders considers "existent" only those that are able to

> *irradiate a power of exhibition and attraction more powerful than everything else.* [...] what is not advertised, what does not call out to us, what does not display itself, what does not form part of the light of the strategic manipulation of advertising has no power to solicit us, we do not perceive it, we do not hear it, we do not share it, we do not recognise it, we do not use it, we do not consume it; in short: it is *ontologically subliminal,* in the pragmatic sense that *it is not there* (it does not exist).
>
> (Anders, 2007b, pp. 145–146)

Ad-vertere, in Latin, means "to turn" (*vertere*) towards (*ad*), the essence of advertising being exactly to capture our attention, and to turn it towards the ad-vertised commodity.

All products want to be taken into consideration, in Anders' words, and display themselves in order to become more visible, and more attractive, than others. Accordingly, our world has become "an advertising exposition, which is impossible not to visit, because we always find ourselves in the middle of it" (Anders, 2007b, p. 146), a multitude of products and objects ad-vertising, that is, "turning our attention towards" themselves.

From the point of view of the product and the commodity, *advertere* may as well correspond to *seducere*, to seduce, to conduct (*ducere*) the user out of their path, towards the product itself. Seduction, in a sexual sense, is the essence of contemporary advertising: every object, every product, every service, every commodity displays itself in a seductive way, trying to attract us towards it. Se-duction is necessary for pro-duction.

In a similar way, politicians have to seduce the electorate, no matter how miserable that template may be, from some points of view. The so-called "seduction of the candidates" has become much more important than the often negligible, and not rarely mendacious, contents of the actual political proposals. Politicians and political ideas have become products and brands to be marketed and "bought" by unwary electors. The leading Western exponent of such political marketing is the United States of America, since the 1960 debates for the presidential election between John Fitzgerald Kennedy and Richard Nixon, in the CBS studios in Chicago.

The best model in nature, that is of sexual seduction, has been taken as the scaffolding of the whole advertising industry, and has been applied to any good or product. That the female body and its powerful, seductive image have come under the aegis of the advertising industry is no surprise at all, and the transformation of sexual seduction into seductive qualities of commodities has gone hand in hand with decreasing taboos and prejudices regarding sexual matters during the second half of the twentieth century.

Certainly, the change in morality and sexual behaviours is a complex phenomenon, and must be considered as the result of several interacting factors, over a wide timescale: in the course of centuries, the history of Western consciousness arrived at the "death of God", the repression of limits, the fading of patriarchal values, the sunset of the father principle, and all these factors and more contributed to wide-ranging changes in morality, sexuality, and gender claims for equality, as we will see in Chapter Five. Still these changes received a great amount of assistance from the commercial reality too.

If the Western world appears nowadays "pornified", it's not because of porn, but because of this commercial reality. The term *advertising* has a synonym in the word *publicity*. *Publicus, in Latin,* refers to what belongs to everybody, to the people: what is exposed to everyone's glance, is *public*. "Public woman" meant in fact prostitute, and the contiguity of this term with the exposition in public of products and services can be here considered in its erotic valence.

The producers of commodities and services have basically changed the function of the sexual impulse, transforming it into a demand for their products. Anders maintains that *"being-in-the-advertising-world* represents an ontological *status* of particular kind; that we who live as fellow citizens in an advertising world, are *there* in a different sense than our father and ancestors were *there*; that our lives are played out as an incessant *being courted*" (Anders, 2007, p. 148). To court, to seduce, is what commodities do through their physical appearance and through advertisement: this sexualisation has become a fundamental quality of the world we inhabit, "since our world is a world that *publicises it* [...] And given that nothing is more effective in getting our attention than sexual excitation, the world is no longer presented as the world itself, but as *sirenic*" (Anders, 2007b, pp. 287–288). The image of the sirens, singing loud their chant, attracting us towards them, comes back in Anders' definition. He continues, adding that "the term *publicise* recovers its original sexual meaning. Only, now *we* are not the *subjects* of publicity, but the commodities are (or more precisely, the producers of the commodities), who zealously hunt for customers, that is, they must display themselves as exciting objects. *They are there, rank upon rank, to conquer us in our capacity as buyers*" (Anders, 2007b, pp. 288–289).

Therefore, the pornification of the world, as Pamela Paul dubs it, appears to be much more a consequence of the erotisation of the world due to the seductive needs of the productive apparatus, in order to produce needs in the consumers, than an effect of porn and its pervasiveness. The idea of a world *clothed in nudity*, as Anders brilliantly summarises, aptly describes the immense market we dwell in, a market where we are not looking at commodities, rather we are looked at by them, and by their advertising, seductive images.

This is the landscape we wander about in, a mass of millions of coerced voyeurs, encouraged to become addicted, as described in the previous chapters. This landscape was solidly established during the whole course of the twentieth century, and only when the "law" of the *sexual seduction of the products* was firmly rooted in our reality, formal laws and legal acts enabled the production and the distribution of porn material; as previously mentioned, this happened only during the last thirty years of the twentieth century. Thanks to the spreading of new technological devices, porn started circulating more and more, eventually becoming itself a successful product displayed on the world's shelves.

What I mean to say is that porn became more available when the pornification of the world was already a *fait accompli*. Subsequently, porn *imaginarium* returned back to the commercial reality, informing its visual language: from fashion magazines to street adverts, women embodied the intensely seductive energy of porn images, their glance in the camera, hinting at unbelievable pleasures, biting or licking their slightly open lips, their bodies as juicy and thrilling as those of porn actresses, with an increasing use of lesbo poses, for instance, no matter what product or service is advertised.

The music industry, like any other industry, has been affected by the same return: especially during the 1980s and 1990s, female pop-rock stars increasingly assumed porn-like poses, dresses, and attitudes, obviously to sell their albums and their very image; in rap music, the porn-slut female became an enduring part of the rappers' pantheon of values, together with big money, expensive cars, golden necklaces, and diamond-studded rings.

In the era of social networks, unsurprisingly the portraits people upload as their profile pictures share the same codes as porn pics, in order to advertise themselves, one would be tempted to say, to be visible, to gain clicks, and a sense of existence online, as we will later explore.

Actually, in the current scenario, porn products could be seen as the only ones that appropriately make use of sexual seduction as a way to attract attention, as the products are themselves sexual. Legs, tits, asses used to advertise a car, a drill, a holiday, or an insurance company are much more deceitful and dodgy than if they just advertise themselves, and the powerful attraction of sex.

However, only were we getting rid of the openly sexual side of the current exhibition of commodities, the essential seductiveness of every element of our reality, and the fact of being incessantly and inadvertently courted by millions of advertising images and phantoms, would be stably affirmed and re-affirmed.

The two plush pets that opened this chapter, grinning at me from my children's bed, with their big eyes, are there to testify to the powerful implementation of current seductiveness. They were effectively able to turn my child's attention towards them, seducing him, and abusing of, I would dare to say, his natural child's desire to love and be loved by a little pet. This abuse subtly instilled a need in him, renovating a desire that had been already fulfilled by other plush pets, and eventually compelled us to buy him another one. I reckon this abusive side of products' seduction and of the advertisement industry is particularly hideous.

Porn can surely be considered an uncanny object on the shelves, but it's the whole, invisible supermarket itself, the trademark of our capitalistic and technological world, wrapping us up with its apparently innocuous coils, that unsettles me to the utmost.

CHAPTER FOUR

Porn and the roses of Kenya

Every day, a beautiful rose flies from Kenya, in the company of several tons of other roses, scented and colourful travel mates, heading to Holland.[1] After being transported from Schiphol airport, this immense amount of roses gathers in the largest building in footprint of the entire world,[2] located in the small municipality of Aalsmeer. Every day, hundreds of trucks collect those very roses from Aalsmeer, and transport them all over Europe. Every day, some of them, cut and prepared, travel back to Schiphol airport, in order to depart by plane towards the US market, or to Japan.

In the improbable case that a rose bought in Helsinki, the city where I live, does not come from Kenya, it probably comes from Colombia, after having sojourned anyway in Aalsmeer, and slept all the way in one of the dozens of trucks travelling daily from Holland up to Finland.

Reportedly, Aalsmeer gained a sinister reputation for its Nazi support during the Second World War. I coincidentally found this information on Wikipedia, and was surprised, as this news was perfectly in tune with my pre-existent intention to outline an inconvenient inheritance that Nazism left to the Western world. In the project of the extermination camps, national socialism brought the division of labour, the specialisation of work, and the lack of conscience of the final goals to the highest levels of perfection.

Seizing, registering, and collecting millions of prisoners in transition camps all over Europe, preparing a capillary network of train trips heading to the camps from different nations, skimming the possible workers, and sending them daily out of the camps to be exploited by war and civil industries, supplying the camps themselves with all the victuals and necessary goods that had to be produced and delivered from elsewhere (including the notorious Zyklon B for the gas chambers), were carefully coordinated activities that required a much larger number of people than the soldiers and employees attending at the industrious production of corpses in the camps.

In this regard, Günther Anders wonders who is not familiar with the ill-reputed answer "I was only doing my duty!", given by everyone accused of participating, in some form or degree, in the terrible crimes perpetuated by national socialism. The various workers in the chemical factories producing Zyklon B, for instance, those who were storing it, those who were delivering it, the accountants and the employees of all the factories, their directors, managers, and so on, could authentically feel they were just doing what was asked them, their duty, their job, precisely because they were requested to concentrate only on their small part of the process. The bigger picture, the complexity of the whole process, and most of all, its final, deadly goal, were (encouraged to be) out of their awareness.

However horrible this may sound, even the employees within the camps, who were witnessing that final goal and actively participating in it, even, did not feel they "acted", rather they just "worked", obeying superior orders.

Anders suggests an interesting distinction between "to act" and "to work/to do". The first verb may refer to actions we undertake, being aware of and responsible for their consequences, acknowledging and taking these into account. "To work/to do", by contrast, may refer to the mere performance of a duty, disconnected from its ultimate consequences, the absence of any moral conscience being a constitutive element of the job that has to be done.

"To work/to do", in such a system, is possible thanks to labour division, where each specialised worker is responsible only for the result of the task to which he or she has been assigned. The final goal, with which he or she *de facto* cooperates, is not his or her business. Accordingly, there can be neither sense of responsibility for it, nor shame or guilt. In other words, each worker is reduced to a mere human cog of a bigger mechanism, whose logic and aims can be easily ignored, or better, they have to be ignored. The job has to be done, no matter what, how, or for what reason.

After the end of the Second World War, each person accused of participating in the criminal plan of extermination basically felt as a mere subordinate, claiming that he or she could not have acted in any other way. The only moral to stick to was that of doing a good job, as testified by Eichmann himself, in the lucid portrait made of him by Hanna Arendt (1963).

I dared to dub all this an "inconvenient inheritance", as the inner logic perfected by national socialism has been brilliantly assimilated by the current dominant corporate mentality, and by global capitalism.

As a matter of fact, almost any activity ("to act") has been transformed into operating ("to work/to do"), and almost any operating has been transformed into cooperating, devoid of any responsibility and awareness of its implications and consequences. Under this perspective, many of the jobs and activities we are doing in our current world seem dominated by the same "de-responsibilisation", and each of us is more or less inadvertently (or, in some cases, knowingly and enthusiastically, even) coopted to cooperate with goals that may be disputable, if not blatantly harmful.

The scenario that opens this chapter, for instance, is somehow apocalyptic, seen from the environmental point of view. I wonder who could maintain that for the sake of buying a rose in Helsinki, billions of oil should be consumed by the thousands of planes, cargos, and trucks employed for carrying every single day tons of roses from Kenya to Europe, heavily polluting the atmosphere. As simple as it is, buying a rose contributes to destroying our planet.

But if a jury were to raise the accusation of planet destruction against any of the workers employed in the process, from those who cultivate the roses to those who collect them, from those who pack them to those who deliver them to Holland, from those who prepare them to those who transport them everywhere, from all the employees involved at each stage of the process to the managers, the accountants, the lawyers of the companies, from the marketing managers to the flower shop sellers, they all would claim: "I was only doing my job!" Each of them would ignore the ultimate consequences of what they are doing, that is, what they are requested to do, or supposed to do: their small part of a bigger process.

Besides, the final consumer is as equally involved, a cog like any other in the process; in fact, his or her existence as a buyer ensures the continuation and expansion of the whole project, as previously mentioned. Accordingly, the role of the consumers is absolutely essential. From the environmental perspective, buying a rose may be seen as an act of involuntary cooperation in the destruction of the planet.

We all, as buyers of any kind of product, could be accused of contributory negligence, and of being co-respondent for such a crime. Considering that the example of rose trading is an almost negligible element, and not even the worst, in the wider landscape of the current world market, where goods and commodities keep travelling vortically around the planet, produced, transported, bought, consumed, and wasted away, may cause dizziness. As a matter of fact, the twentieth century has definitely shaped a world in which almost no action is innocuous. Buying food from the supermarkets is not at all a harmless action, considering the logic of global trading that completely ignores environmental sustainability. Eating in fast-food restaurants or sushi bars is more obviously grievous, but every form of restaurant business is culpable to some degree. Buying toys, clothes, technological products, travelling low or high cost, enjoying most of the leisure activities we are offered, owning and using cars and other private means of transportation, are all less than innoxious actions. And most of our jobs are inherently implicated as well.

The ultimate consequences of our current way of being-in-the-world as mandatory consumers and cogs of bigger mechanisms, in terms of destruction of the sea and the land, exploitation of natural resources and people, support to criminal regimes and groups of economic power, lack of respect for the rights of workers, minorities, children, animals, and so on, would nail the majority of us to very big responsibilities, by virtue of our cooperation and correspondence.

Many forms of resistance to this apparently more or less compulsory cooperation are gaining strength and visibility, in several countries, and contribute to bringing about more awareness, but the complexity and the dimensionality of the phenomena we are outlining here is such that grazing them seems to require titanic efforts.[3]

As an infinitely duplicable and reproducible technological product on the shelves of the world supermarket, and as a symbol of our current *zeitgeist*, porn is, once again, necessarily subjected to the same logic as any other mass-produced goods.

In the second chapter, we have seen how the world is mostly supplied to us through its images, or *phantoms*. Magazines, radio, television, and, in the last two decades, the World Wide Web deliver to us images of the world to be consumed, as products and services in their own right. Able to access them at any time, simply connecting to the internet, we are transformed into permanent voyeurs, this transformation being essential particularly with regard to porn, as the sex scene is filmed *for* the spectator, having him in mind: it exists for him.

The transformation or, as previously dubbed, the reduction of the consumer into a voyeur/spectator goes hand in hand with his or her cooptation and cooperation, in the meaning outlined in this chapter.

Each individual has his or her own part or role in the chain of tasks composing the process/service called "porn": from the actresses and actors to the camera operator, from the film-maker to the crew (in the increasingly rare case of professional porn industry movies), from the webmasters to the distributors, and so on. The role of the spectator of a porn video or a series of porn pictures, his duty or job, so to say, is to watch the video or the pictures, and hopefully to pay for them. I add "hopefully", because the availability of porn materials on net platforms like xvideos, you porn, porn hub, etc., is basically free. In these free web platforms, thousands of new videos are uploaded every day, from short samples to almost complete scenes, of every genre and kind. These videos can be enjoyed in streaming, or they can be downloaded for free (after logging into the web platform) and saved for a rainy day, but the explicit hope is that the consumer enrols, paying a monthly fee, for accessing the original website and many other satellite webpages.[4]

The consumer may pay or not pay for what he watches, still he accomplishes his part of the process, his job: he is turned into a voyeur and a collaborator (*cum-laborare*; etymologically the one who does the work, the labour, the job, *cum*, that is, together), dismissed from feeling responsible for the whole process and its possible consequences. He can blissfully ignore what happened before and after the porn scene, most of all the physical or psychological price paid by the actresses. That is not his business. The consumer can concentrate on his part of the job, that is, to be entertained at someone else's expense, like in almost any other field of our complex society.

In the next chapter, we will explore the increasingly extreme nature of porn performances, understanding this tendency as reflecting the general direction the Western world has trodden since the Industrial Revolution; according to one's own character, psychological type, subjective experiences, values, and frames of meaning, porn materials may reach the point when they become extremely shocking or disturbing. Coming myself across a particularly brutal gang bang scene, I intensely felt how unacceptable it can be to find yourself forced into the role of co-respondent, collaborator to something you do not want to happen.[5] A similar feeling of impotence I had felt about the roses from Kenya and their unspoken price for the whole planet arose from the passive experience of these kinds of porn scenes.

Of course, as I can avoid buying a rose, I can avoid watching porn scenes that exceed my degree of acceptance, shirking from the passive role assigned to me as cooperating voyeur/spectator. In other words, I can oppose an "action" to the servile "job" I am requested and supposed to do.

Still, roses are cultivated, transported, distributed, and sold, and porn as well is filmed, uploaded, seen, and sold.

Would my rebellion against the tame role of cooperating consumer be of any use, in a deeper way, in questioning the general dominating model of our technological and capitalistic world, that is, the division of labour, the specialisation of the workers, the cancellation of the awareness of the final goals and the bigger pictures, and the consequent shameful refusal of responsibility?

May I call myself somehow out of this global mechanism?

But, most of all, is there still an "out"?

CHAPTER FIVE

Porn and no limit

In another work of mine, I have pointed out how the repression of limit could be regarded as one of the core elements of Western societies.[1]

This repression may be considered the outcome of a long process, the upshot of the internal logic of the history of the Western world, as Martin Heidegger put it, until the essence of the philosophical thought of the eighteenth and nineteenth centuries, together with the increasing power of the scientific-technological apparatus, made a growing domination of technology over every aspect of human life possible. Enlightenment and the Industrial Revolution fostered a progressive repression of limits, and paved the way to a pervasive omnipotent mentality: in fact, the pre-conditions for technology to expand infinitely its potential to reach goals are the sunset of every absolute truth, the decay of immutable principles, and the disappearance of any metaphysical limit.

It's a terrific passage in the course of the history of consciousness, or better, a rupture, that Nietzsche clearly detected and expressed while it was occurring, with his famous statement that God was dead, and that all the supreme values had lost every value.[2]

The scientific and technological impulse moved on through the course of the twentieth century, following the implicit motto "everything that can be done, must be done", regardless of any form of limitation, thus reaching an apparent domination of nature. The latter has been ultimately considered nothing more than *materia* to be exploited and ransacked, with the physical limits of the planet we inhabit basically ignored.

The immense production apparatus aims at perpetuating and expanding itself, as previously stated, turning everyone into its unpaid employee, while the dominant economic theories are often, if not always, based on a model of infinite growth, their recent history being a constant advancement towards a condition of limitlessness and boundlessness: turbo-capitalism, economic liberalism, consumerism essentially proceed according to what I would dub the "inner logic of cancer", an infinite growth and expansion, regardless the environmental conditions of the body they inhabit.

During the last decades, in addition, mobile phones, computers, tablets, the internet, and the cyber world have unceasingly expanded our sensation of limitlessness, constantly feeding an unswerving omnipotent mentality.

This doesn't just affect the economic and technological fields; medicine as well pursues an ideal of health as a state of (actually impossible) absence of any malady; while various psychologies are equally preaching the "ten steps to wellbeing, happiness, and balance", suggesting that everything is possible, if one just willingly follows the right methods and techniques.

In the current age of mass communication, advertisement is probably the main element nurturing the idea of repression of limits, since almost any slogan can be reduced to the basic message that "you can/anything is possible, whoever you are" ("if you buy this object/this service", obviously). Feeding this collective omnipotent mentality goes hand in hand with advertisement's fundamental role in producing our needs, as depicted in the previous chapters.

In summary, we all are daily immersed and swimming in such an omnipotent mentality, in almost every area of our lives; it's no surprise if this repression of limits includes old age, and most of all the supreme limit we all have to acknowledge and face, that is, death.[3]

Like entwined threads in Western history's rope, the process of nurturing an omnipotent mentality has gone together with the unrelenting decline of the father principle,[4] traditionally representing the limit and the law, and with the emersion from any previous form of mythical, religious, and metaphysical frame that has contained humankind for many millennia.[5]

A single individual may still feel him- or herself contained in some frame of meaning, even a religious one, in Western societies; but the gap between how the individual feels and perceives their way of being-in-the-world, and how the collective level has turned out to be over more than two centuries, is actually a primary, and inadequately explored, issue of our current era. On one side, we have human beings, with their beliefs, and acute need of frames of meaning, while on the other, the world they inhabit has long ago become fatherless, godless, frameless, limitless, technological, and functional.

This gap may be dramatically and painfully reduced when a limit suddenly appears, for instance in the form of an unexpected or premature death, a heavily disabling illness, the loss of someone important, an insight into our extreme vulnerability, or some acute or ongoing traumatic experience. These are the moments when an individual may find him- or herself utterly unarmed, and devoid of any tools to face and to cope with these limits. The illusory curtain of a seemingly eternal, safe, and entertained life is miserably torn into pieces, and the threat of darkness blatantly appears in the most devastating ways.

Indeed, many are the psychological consequences of living immersed in such a no-limit mentality. For the sake of this work, we may at least point out how acknowledging and confronting the limit has always been a necessary element in the process of building up what C. G. Jung called the ego complex.

Limit comes from the Latin word *limes*, which originally meant "border, boundary". The experience of my limits, thus, corresponds to becoming aware of my boundaries and borders, aware of where "me" ends and the other begins, in other words, aware of who I am. First, the prevailing attitude of repression of limit may deprive many of us of the possibility of developing a solid and sufficiently rooted sense of identity. What the sociologist Zygmunt Bauman dubs "liquid identity" may be seen as the result of this very deprivation. Undoubtedly, a liquid identity is more capable of adapting to the constant changes of our modern reality; still, it might imply an uncanny feeling of not being grounded and rooted, and this in turn might profoundly affect our sense of existence.

Accordingly, when borders and boundaries are felt as evanescent and vague, a sense of existence may rather come from *visibility*. I am seen, *ergo* I exist, one may say: visibility becomes the cypher of existence, and the most craved status, by the inhabitants of the liquid modernity. Moreover, this deep need happens to fit perfectly the possibly infinite offer of visibility supplied by the technological devices of our cyber world. In this regard, the World Wide Web may be perceived as a sort of immense, democratic stage where each of us can be seen, heard, and read, in social networks, websites, video channels, and so on, thus having at least a glimpse of existence. Everyone may easily satisfy their own pangs of visibility, although always subjected to the relentless law of the like/dislike function, a sort of universal Judgement of the current times.

I reckon this need to be seen in order to feel that one exists might play an important, albeit unconscious, role in the increasing amount of *amateur* porn videos and pictures uploaded on the web by users all over the world, as well as in the professional activity of porn performers, who can obtain global visibility, some kind of notoriety, in the niche of the sex world, and some economic success.

As a matter of fact, since its birth, porn has been entwined with the topic of breaking the limits, those of morality and of common decency *in primis*. By its very existence, porn immediately started challenging, trespassing, and moving these limits forward, since the first pictures and movies of the nineteenth century. Interestingly enough, this was made possible only thanks to women who happened to live abundantly beyond those limits, being in most cases prostitutes.

Porn pictures and short movies, just like a subterranean river, flowed through the course of the twentieth century in the shadow of the depths, until they started streaming more openly, in the outdoors, together with the manifold social changes of the 1960s. The fading of patriarchal values, the growing need of gender equality for women all over the Western world, their struggle for the right to vote and participate in the political and economical life of their countries, which had begun by the end of the nineteenth century, along with women's emancipation from their traditional roles as wives and mothers, submissive to the authority of a male, their right to make decisions about their own bodies, and about sexual desire as well, the separation between sexuality and its reproductive function, the process of gaining greater self-determination, these were all fundamental phenomena that evolved in synchrony with the spreading of porn materials.

The development of and the interactions between all these phenomena would constitute too complex a topic, while easy causalisms between porn and these societal changes would be at best naive and simplifying. Nevertheless, through the swinging sixties, porn certainly mingled with the subversion of bourgeois morality and values, and with the sexual revolution, until it obtained legal right to be produced and distributed, in the end of the decade.

The Danish movies of this period, and a good proportion of the production of porn movies throughout the 1970s, in the United States, in Sweden, and in France, are often imbued with the enthusiasm of expanding the horizons of sex, exploring the extreme, and especially showing women experiencing their sexuality freely and joyfully, after millennia of patriarchal oppression, restrictions, and limitations.

The opening scene of what can be considered the first mass porn movie in history, *Deep Throat*,[6] may be seen as a symbol of this new and subversive perspective on women: we see Linda Lovelace, the main actress, driving alone in a big, beautiful old American car, through the streets of Miami, for several minutes, while titles and names scroll. Keeping in mind that it was 1972, already this long sequence gives a flavour of autonomy and self-determination. Linda gets home, only to find her friend Helen, sitting on the kitchen counter, her legs wide open, while a man on his knees does her a *cunnilingus*. Helen speaks naturally to Linda, while enjoying what is going on, the man being represented as a diligent tool for her pleasure.

When Helen lights up a cigarette, she cares to ask him, "Do you mind if I smoke, while you are eating?" (intending her pussy) and the man replies gently "Not at all!". The camera focuses for a long time on Helen's sexual enjoyment, and her satisfied facial expressions, more than on her genitals. These first minutes of the movie appear to be a powerful statement of women's right to pleasure, and Linda Lovelace also portrays the character of a young woman who is looking for a deeper and more satisfying sexual experience, resembling a quest for a spiritual ecstasy, or of totality.

But together with these subversive elements, we can at the same time notice the centrality of a male sexual perspective in the main fictional point of the simple plot: Linda is unable to reach a complete orgasm, until her doctor finds out her clitoris is not placed in the vulva, but deep down her throat. Linda discovers that she can actually experience a bursting pleasure (funnily represented by images of bells ringing, fireworks exploding in the sky, and a space rocket roaring on a launching pad, even) only via extreme blow jobs, with the total insertion of the penis in her mouth, in order to stimulate directly her clit.[7]

The newborn attitudes of women's sexual liberation, and the hitherto unheard right of women to seek their own pleasure, were immediately mingled with a more traditional male perspective on sex and women's role, since this very first mass porn movie.

As soon as porn films and magazines turned out to be a remunerative good to be produced and sold within the law, the initially enthusiastic attitude of joyful enjoyment of sexuality left room to a variety of genres, that is, products intended for men's pleasure, which turned immediately towards the extreme, already during the 1970s. In turn, coherently with the general omnipotent frame that colours the lives of each of us in Western societies, as previously mentioned, the aim of trespassing moral limits and sexual norms veered quickly into a more extreme denial, or repression, of limit in the sexual performances.

The sociologist Pietro Adamo points out in his work (2004) that the collapse of the Soviet Union, and the rapid changes and consequent turmoil in all the ex country-members of the Warsaw Pact, introduced into the porn market during the 1990s a huge number of young girls and women in need of money, and willing to do absolutely anything to earn it.

At the same time, the advent of the internet has had a deep impact on the whole porn market: the professional porn movie industry was sidelined by thousands of smaller companies, able to produce movies, clips, and scenes in high volumes with significantly lower costs, and a with capillary distribution via the web. Professional porn performers, with their established rules, rights, and unions even, had to adapt quickly to the new codexes of porn scenes, shot with non-professional or semi-professional actors and actresses. The main concept of the porn movie itself, with some sort of plot, costumes, and not only sexual acting, became just one of the dozens of genres and products in the pornscape, superseded in terms of popularity by shorter sex performances, with no conventional acting, no dialogues, and no plot at all. In addition, the web increasingly encouraged the active uploading of *amateur* materials, which in time has become a genre in its own right, particularly appreciated because of its proximity to possible everyday-life experiences.

The just mentioned cohort of girls and women willing to do absolutely anything, mainly coming from Hungary, the Czech Republic, Ukraine, Belarus, and Russia, teamed up with the growing dominance of the internet and the web, with their ubiquity, limitlessness, and relative anonymity, and led to a much higher degree of extremity in porn imagery, making it the norm.[8]

The no-limits mentality, thus, has radically coloured porn performances, and it could not be different, since this very mentality imbues basically every field of our current world.

Certainly, the extreme featured in porn movies from the very start, from the end of the 1960s and during the 1970s; still, in the beginning, it was pursued within a general climate of experimentation, and of a consciously aimed subversion of the traditional norms and values, in terms of sexuality, morality, and gender relationships. Conversely, the extent to which limits are trespassed in current mainstream porn is unattainable, and this phenomenon has no other aim than creating a variety of appealing products and brands to be sold in the huge pornscape market: going towards some form of extreme is nowadays the main choice, in order to stand out from an increasing mass of similar products.[9]

Transgression comes from the Latin verb *transgredire*, which means "to go beyond, through", hence the etymological meaning of the word requires a border, a limit to go beyond/to break through. Certainly, transgression has been *ab initio* the essence of porn pictures and movies, and definitely the 1960s' and 1970s' movies represented extremely strong transgressions, which forced the legislation of the Western countries to conceive laws, acts, and rules that redefined the concept of licit.

But in the current, general context, where limits have faded, if not collapsed, porn cannot be any more transgressive according to the etymological meaning, because there is no clear limit, border, or rule to trespass. Actually, to deny limits has become the rule, thus porn cannot any longer represent a transgression.

A very interesting and important point, in this regard, is to acknowledge that the progressive denial of limits in heterosexual porn pertains mainly women, and can be reached only if, when, and how women allow it to happen.

As a matter of fact, the codexes and schema of men's role in porn have not changed much since the very beginning of mass porn: the male performer basically had back then, and has today, just to endure erection, to penetrate (on a continuum, from gently to brutally), and to ejaculate. Nothing transgressive, no limits to trespass, or even repress at all: male sexuality in porn is as transgressive as a tax-form to be filled in.

Basically, the female performer is the one on whose skin the denial of limits topic unfolds, in an escalation whose brink is pretty arduous to define. It could be extremely disturbing and uncanny for the neophyte explorer of the pornscape to come across scenes, which are more and more common in the mainstream porn videos, where a girl or a woman acts *as if* almost anything is possible.[10]

The most radical anti-porn activists find this escalation towards the extreme a perfect subject to support their contempt and hatred for porn, as seen as a degrading, humiliating activity for girls and women, who are blatantly demeaned and compelled to undergo the most pleasureless, brutal, and hideous practices, at the hands of violent, dominating, and unsightly men, who are essentially the perfect caricature of the patriarchal idiot.

This perspective certainly captures one of the most visible colours of the kaleidoscope that porn exhibits: the evident drift, in the last two decades, towards the old, die-hard model of a dominant, even brutal, man, or group of men, submitting a pliable girl or woman, apparently happy (or resigned) to be mistreated, used, and abused. Reckoning porn a much more complex phenomenon, and a manifold symbol of our current era, we are trying to widen the lens to include further perspectives, in order to capture more colours than this ostensibly distressing one.

CHAPTER SIX

Porn and shadow

C. G. Jung's term "shadow" is an evocative image, expressing the destiny of those contents that are repressed and denied, thus excluded from consciousness by the individual (personal shadow), or by the group he or she belongs to, the society, or the culture as a whole (collective shadow).

Post-Jungian authors have written many works about the shadow, essentially analysing shadow figures as they appear in myths, fairy tales, religions, and dreams, and underlining their potentially transformative effect, were they acknowledged and integrated.

Jung believed the personal shadow to be the dark, negative side of our personality: "[it] represents first and foremost the personal unconscious, and its content can therefore be made conscious without too much difficulty" (Jung, 1959, p. 10). A parallel with the Freudian unconscious can be drawn here, as the personal shadow would correspond to contents, desires, phantasies, and needs, considered negative in terms of the values of the society or the culture that the caregivers convey.

The repressed elements tend to manifest themselves first of all in the form of projections, thus the individual can continue ignoring them as part of his or her own psychic landscape, and keep on fighting them in those who carry their projections. Were these projections recognised as such, the person could eventually withdraw them, at least partially, and undergo a process of integration of his or her own negative sides.

Easy to describe in words, this is actually a painful and unsettling process, as Jung aptly maintained:

> The shadow is a moral problem that challenges the whole ego-personality, for no one can become conscious of the shadow without considerable moral effort. To become conscious of it involves recognising the dark aspects of the personality as present and real. This act is the essential condition for any kind of self-knowledge, and it therefore, as a rule, meets with considerable resistance.
>
> (Jung, 1959, p. 8)

Self-knowledge, and what Jung called the process of individuation, may start from the painful, wearisome, and often destabilising encounter with the dark aspects of our own personality.

Also, those elements and contents that a group, a society, or an entire culture consider negative, despicable, and dangerous, the so-called "collective shadow", are often projected onto another group, society, or culture, as masterfully and dramatically described by René Girard in his famous work about the scapegoat mechanism (Girard, 1986).

Conceived as such, the personal and collective shadow are intertwined, as the former is highly dependent on the collective consciousness, that is, the norms and the values of the culture and the society in which the individual lives. This means that its contents are perceived as negative exactly in relation to those norms and values, but they may not necessarily be negative in themselves. A simple, paradoxical example may be that of a child raised within a criminal community, who may be encouraged to repress empathy, kindness, altruism: these and other contents, unaccepted and disciplined by the caregivers, may rightly become part of his or her own shadow, without being "negative" in their absolute value. Nevertheless, many aspects commonly belonging to the shadow, such as jealousy, possessiveness, envy, selfishness, sloth, indifference, wrath, unkindness, cruelty, and so on, are fairly intended as negative.

According to Jung, the deeper we delve into our psyche, the more we come across elements that essentially belong to all human beings, whatever their own life experiences, and the same happens at the core of the personal and collective shadow. These elements, described as archetypal, speak to us of radical evil as an original element of human existential nature, with a voice to which it is extremely difficult to listen. In fact, Jung warned us that "it is quite within the bounds of possibility for a man to recognise the relative evil of his nature, but it is a rare and shattering experience for him to gaze into the face of absolute evil" (Jung, 1959, p. 10). The archetypal, collective aspects of the shadow may represent a terrible challenge, in the uneasy dialogue between our ego and the unconscious.

Being an image, rather than a concept, the shadow possesses soft edges and a foggy nature that should always invite us to reflect more deeply, and most of all, to avoid simplifications, while dealing with it. Personal, collective, and archetypal levels of the shadow entwine and refer to each other in manifold nuances, composing quite a complex landscape to explore.

Talking about porn, we necessarily face shadow aspects, as it directly concerns elements that Western culture has always tried to repress, suppress, deny, or at least regulate for more than two thousand years: sexuality, desire, the body, and the feminine.[1]

These aspects have been, often violently, exiled in the shadow, and reckoned as inferior aspects of human existence,[2] bringing an impoverished, heavily one-sided perspective that magnified the *logos*, the Spirit, the light of rationality, and the (patriarchal) culture, to the detriment of *eros*, the matter, the flesh, and nature. TePaske reminds us that "the patriarchies of Christianity or Judaism—in blatant disregard for the deep connection between religion and sexuality—have failed to provide adequate images, symbols, mythologies, or rituals through which the full range of sexual instincts might be accepted, positively valued, reflected upon, and imaginatively cultivated" (TePaske, 2008, p. 3).

Indeed, porn, a Western invention, concerns the very shadow of the Western culture.

Like the naked emperor in H. C. Andersen's famous short tale, porn is often as visible and present as it is untold and denied. Before the internet and free wi-fi allowed everyone to watch porn whenever they wanted and wherever they were, every standard hotel was including porn movies via pay-TV in the list of normal room services, ensuring that this was billed discreetly at checkout.

An Italian idiom captures the common situation around porn as "Pulcinella's secret" (sometimes referred to in English as "Punchinello's secret"), a secret that is not a secret at all, since everybody knows it. Not only has porn coloured with its inner logic Western fashion, advertisement, art, music videos, entertainment, and many other fields, in the last thirty years, as previously mentioned,[3] but most of all, its presence is barely concealed behind a very thin curtain of denial, naivete, and more often hypocrisy.

Since the late 1970s, the majority of men, from their early teenage years to old age, have watched porn, or watch it regularly for masturbating, without being labelled as perverted or becoming addicted. As a matter of fact, statistical research based on the use of the internet reveal this data clearly,[4] and it's quite amazing how many women seem to be totally unaware of it, until they accidentally find it out.[5]

The pain generated by this discovery seems to be directly proportional to the degree of denial of the (poorly hidden) evidence that porn is actually part of the lives of third-millennium men, unless personal phobias, strong religious or moral beliefs, or rigid norms prevent or inhibit the attraction towards it (repressing it in the shadow, moreover, with psychological consequences worth exploring).

Despite the evidence that most men know a lot about internet porn, its jargon, its definitions, the shelves and the products they can find on the web, in almost two decades of clinical practice, a male patient telling me spontaneously something about his familiarity with porn has been the rarest event. Speaking about sexuality in the consulting room is usually not a taboo, and even talking about masturbation is quite commonly possible and acceptable. But the number of patients telling me something more detailed about their relation to internet porn has been negligible, so far. This sort of taboo seems particular to the use of internet porn, and we know from Freud that where there is a taboo, there is a desire.

Some female colleagues of mine report that in the rare cases when a man had openly spoken to them about porn preferences, fantasies, netporn surfing, and so on, those were narcissistic patients blatantly trying to embarrass, provoke, or unrealistically seduce the therapist.

I tend to believe that the topic of porn is openly dealt with only in those cases when the patient labels himself as porn-addicted, and the mutually agreed aim of the therapy is curing his addictive abuse of internet porn.

Actually, exploring more closely which personal and collective shadow aspects could be revealed in experiencing porn movies and pictures may be fundamental for those who wish to comprehend this complex symbol of our times: for the scholar of social and psychological phenomena, as for the layman; for the therapists who, together with their patients, walk along their path of individuation, as for the patients themselves; for every man who wishes to understand more about his desires and about himself, as for the wounded woman who just found out her husband or boyfriend regularly watches porn on the net.[6]

The first shadow aspect we may outline here concerns a both culturally and individually repressed content: the fact that each of us, as human beings, is a *desiring multiplicity*. As a matter of fact, porn offers an easy, virtual possibility of achieving some form of satisfaction of the naturally manifold world of our desires, albeit in a vicarious way.[7] Acknowledging that we are inhabited by multiple and often contradictory desires has been prevented by millennia of cultural norms, which witnessed the emergence of the monogamous family as the basic "molecule" to build up the social structures of past eras, in the Western world.

The topic of the repression of our multiply desiring nature is too complex to be explored here in a deeper way.[8] Let's be content to note that this topic has always had to do with the need of the ego to keep some control, during the process of its emergence, of the uncontrollable par excellence, that is, sexual drive.[9]

Also, this topic has had to do with the strong need of past societies to maintain some kind of stability, whose outcome has always turned into a complex and more or less rigid set of norms and rules about relationships, sexuality, and marriage. And it has had to do with the numinous nature of sexuality, that placed it in dangerous contiguity with the sacred, whose monopoly and strict administration have been pursued by all the forms of religion.

But in the current, limitless capitalistic and technological world, isolated individuals with multiple desires have gained much more value than in any previous era. Needs and desires are not only enormously encouraged, but even produced, as previously mentioned, as their (always partial) fulfilment and satisfaction is the very fuel of an endless production, in our consumerist society.

Although the conflict between inner desires and external rules is dissolving on a collective level, under the pressure of the free market, on the individual level, imbued as we are by two thousand years of Christian precepts, the repression of our desiring multiplicity is still a problematic issue. Speaking of couple relationships, for example, it is easier for the majority of individuals to acknowledge their own manifold desires than to admit the existence of the same multiplicity in their partners.

Within patriarchal societies, permission for some form of sexual satisfaction outside marriage (which implicitly refers to the acknowledged presence of multiple desires) has always been the sole prerogative of men. The aforementioned repression of sexuality, the body, and the feminine gave strength to powerful needs, and to an inner conflictuality that has had its hidden forms of resolution or compromise, at least regarding men, while the social shame deriving from the discovery of these hidden forms has been falling mostly on women.

The feminist struggle for equality and the separation of sexuality from the reproductive function have opened, at last, the possibility for acknowledging the same desiring multiplicity in women as well, albeit its ways of unfolding might differ from those of the masculine.

On one, negative, hand, capitalism and consumerism benefit very much from these broadened possibilities, turning them into more opportunities for new products and services, disguised as free ways of self-expression, as always. On another, more positive, hand, the fading of all the previous frames of meaning, the consequent no-limits mentality, and the growing difficulties in looking for a deeper meaning in life and in the experience of our mortality, may awaken a strong need to regain our bodies, our sensorial reality, the sphere of senses and desires, as a foundation of a more balanced way of being in the world. Accordingly, a recovery of the previously repressed desiring multiplicity inhabiting our psyche and of corporeal sensuality, and their integration, could represent a step ahead on a transformative and individuative path, on a personal and on a collective level.

Porn openly shows multiple desires in action, it speaks of enjoying sex with anyone, at any time, everywhere, giving evidence to elements normally exiled in the shadow. For these reasons, porn could have a role in this transformative path, but much more often it is merely turned into (and experienced as) a regressive compulsion, a narcissistic fulfilment, just another product that we must consume, again and again.

Repressed and demonised for two thousand years, as was the previous one, a second shadow aspect possibly conveyed by some kinds of porn is what could be described as a *pristine joy of the body*, that is, a joyous sensation of naturalness, energy, and pleasure in feeling the sensuality of the body.

The lack of judgement about physical appearance, the acceptance of the other, no matter who he or she is, the straightforwardness of the expression of desire, the directness of the sexual exchange, the apparent atmosphere of free enjoyment of sex in any form,[10] may be transmitted to the spectator, who, at times, can feel energised, resonating with an excitement that is more than sexual. I would describe it as *a joyful feeling of being an excited and responding body*, in sharp contrast with the more usual thought of *having* a body: a body that must satisfy the aesthetic requests of advertisement and fashion, a body that has to perform, to be slim, fit, flawless, a machine-body that carries our brains around, a disconnected body.

I believe that this joyful feeling of being, of *embodying our body*, in a sensual (referencing the five senses) and sexual way as well, is the reason why couple therapists may encourage men and women to watch porn movies together, especially when they wish to regain a lost intimacy, desire, and a more confident and disinhibited attitude towards themselves and the partner.

When porn is evoking such pristine joy, masturbation too may be experienced as a healthy, energising relationship with one's own body, a way to care for oneself, and not as a sad, solitary surrogate for sexual intercourse, a sort of tranquilliser for anxiety or depression, a compulsive necessity, and so on. The joyful sensation may persist alongside masturbation, in the form of a more confident feeling of being grounded, more attractive, and living in a world full of possibilities.

The degree of repression in the shadow and the demonisation of this aspect over millennia show how powerful and destabilising it was perceived to be by the traditional patriarchal culture, and by different religions. One patient told me that viewing girls and women in porn had given him many positive sensations, a temporary relief from the difficulties of life, a sense of possibility, and a series of emotions, including admiration, devotion, infatuation for the actresses themselves, and gratitude.

A third, deeper, and more complex shadow side related to porn blatantly speaks of the destructive aspects of our human nature.

Psychoanalysis has taught us that the mysterious and miraculous result of millions years of evolution, that is, the ego, is basically grounded on primary narcissism: identity is thought to be built on will to power, and defines itself in the negative, so to say, on the capacity of destruction and abuse of the other.[11]

Despite millennia of evolution of the soul, human beings at every latitude are still inclined to the abuse of the weak for strengthening their own fragile, empty identities, to the *libido dominandi*, to the violence against the neighbour, the animals, and nature. Capitalism, economic liberalism, consumerism, the exploitation of natural resources, and of people all over the world, are basically the legalised and more acculturated transposition of the very same primal ingredients of our psyche.

Both on the individual and the collective levels, these negative, destructive elements are usually denied, repressed, exiled in the shadow, and eventually projected onto some appointed victim, or scapegoat. Were we acknowledging them as primal ingredients of our own psychological landscape, they would show the radical, archetypal evil in us.

Traditionally, the masculine way of expressing the destructive sides of the psyche is through open aggressiveness, oppression, and physical violence, while the feminine way can be more subtle, less evident, more often played out on a psychological level; however, these generalisations have to take into account all the nuances and mingled features that can be actually embodied by real human beings, whichever biological gender they belong to.

At any rate, it is undeniable that much of contemporary porn shows more and more often men's abusive and violent attitudes towards women. In the last three decades, professional porn actresses and non-professional girls and women in porn had to experience in their very flesh ever more extreme performances, set on a continuum whose upper end keeps moving forward, as we outlined in previous chapters. The extreme end of such a continuum reaches peaks where a woman is literally reduced to mere holes to be brutally penetrated, painfully stretched to the utmost, and besmirched by any possible body fluid, a sort of meek slave of an openly sadistic male satisfaction, or de-animated toy-object that can be used, abused, degraded, humiliated, and despised too.[12]

Some videos indeed do not show just sexual acts, rather they offer an accurate survey of girls and women whilst they are losing their very soul. Towards this pole of the continuum, men do not take delight *together with* a woman, rather *through* her, at her expense. In such cases, a remarkable lack of empathy characterises the male performers, who are moreover convinced that the girls like what they undergo, after all. This point of view emerges quite clearly in books that recount the experiences of male and female porn performers, and it's often blindly accepted and agreed by the average male porn consumer as well, who is in turn convinced by an apparently real representation of "whores in heat", going crazy for what is done to them.

Speaking about a continuum, it is a matter of debate where one might set a point where this particular aspect of destructiveness is seen to emerge. The destructive shadow aspect and the consequent abasement of women's dignity are seen all over the continuum, even at the lower end, by anti-porn feminists and activists, for instance. Men in general, instead, find very exciting girls and women willing to do anything, and the range of this "anything" differs quite substantially from that of women who watch porn materials. In my experience, women detect this destructive aspect much earlier on the continuum than men, while men, especially those who enjoy porn, tend to notice the presence of this aspect only at a much higher level. Accordingly, it would be pretty difficult to set a precise value on the continuum determining when men and women would all agree on a clear emergence of destructive shadow sides. Giving up precision, though, and being well familiar with all the genres, the narratives, and the stylistic elements of current internet porn, it's not impossible to identify some shadow aspects, going from man's selfish sexual satisfaction, increasing lack of responsibility towards the female partners and how they feel, a demeaning attitude, different levels of aggressiveness, clear brutality, up to forthright sadistic violence, and pleasure for the other's humiliation, degradation, and pain.

A patient of mine, with whom I worked for only a few months, had psychopathic traits and a marked lack of awareness of the other's emotions, as well as of his own, and expressed the greatest admiration for male porn actors whose performances were markedly brutal, that is, for the typical patriarchal, macho-like, or unsightly idiots who force the actresses to endure rough, abusive, and humiliating sex scenes, and who seem to enjoy their own harassing ways, and the actresses' pain and disgust.[13] Such scenes show the most hideous domination of the weak, a feature that is typically most appealing to the weakest individuals, those in need of putting the pieces of an evanescent identity together. Watching the pitiable spectacle of wretched, paltry men gaining power through the abuse of a submissive girl, my patient could vicariously himself assume a sense of male power and grandiosity, strengthening his fragile, insubstantial ego, momentarily at least.

Assuming that exerting power over someone is a basic ingredient of our original psychic structure and development implies that this element may resonate in the deep shadow of everyone. Porn offers a very immediate opportunity to get in touch with this element, to feel some degree of resonance in oneself, and to see which emotions are evoked by this discovery. The painful process of individuation, according to Jung, precisely requires us to come into contact without compromise with our shadow aspects, and to do something with what we find out. Ignoring and projecting them, or embodying them thoughtlessly, like my patient did, are not the only possibilities to deal with shadow contents.

Discovering the personal point on the previously sketched continuum could be a very important step in the process of self-knowledge of a man, but also a desirable awareness for his female partner. The individuation process of a post-modern individual would benefit much from meeting the shadow, destructive elements of their own psyche, as hoped by Erich Neumann in his too often unheeded work on the need of a new ethic.[14]

Furthermore, the fact that porn is profoundly entwined with the topic of the shadow is also revealed by what I would define as the *haunting quality* of porn images.

We know from current researches that the average age when a child comes across porn materials on the net is about nine years old. The natural reaction of a child exposed to raw porn images is often disgust. But the reaction of a teenager, as well as that of a more adult person getting in touch with a new, more extreme, shocking porn image or scene, is actually the same: a strong emotional response, often polarised in a negative way.

I maintain that it is the deep resonance with some shadow content of our own psyche that determines the *haunting quality* that a porn image may assume for the viewer. His mind can become obsessed by the shocking image or content, and this obsession, over time, can overturn the initial negative reaction, and force him to look for the same image or scene again. The repeated view of the same unsettling scene often defuses its powerful, haunting presence. Inurement can become the typical outcome of a repeated exposure to something that in the beginning was shocking to some degree (interestingly enough, the Italian word for "inurement", *assuefazione*, is in turn translated into English as "habit" but also "addiction").

What in the beginning had been shocking and disturbing can turn into a persistent, haunting element due to its deeper resonance with some shadow aspect. A mixture of repulsion and fascination, a blend of disgust and curiosity, are usually the strong emotions evoked by this haunting content, until the viewer gives in, and looks for the shocking image again. Inurement results in a reduction of the initial negative emotional reaction, and of the haunting quality of the original content, and in the long run the viewer can come to feel an open attraction to it, even.[15] This whole pattern reveals once again the involvement of shadow elements.

In this chapter, we have tried to enlighten at least some of these elements involved in the experience of watching porn. Our repressed desiring multiplicity and the pristine joy of the body could be considered essentially positive contents, confined in the shadow just because of their subversive and destabilising quality, in relation to the traditional cultural values. The continuum on the scale of destructiveness, in contrast, can be labelled as negative, and it concerns the individual psychic structure of every viewer and his personal history, on the one hand, as well as collective or even archetypal elements speaking of the destructive polarity of our psyche, on the other.

It is important to point out that we have dealt with shadow aspects in relation to the phenomenon of mass porn in every single chapter of this present work. Porn as a technological object clearly embodies the shadows of our society of technology: for instance, its extensive and pervasive domination over our lives; its encouraging in us an addictive attitude to the commodities we produce; the dissociation between ourselves and the physical experience of the world, the dissociation between experiences and emotions, and our reduction to mere spectators and voyeurs of images of the world.

Porn as a mass product on sale on the shelves of the supermarket that surrounds us, shares the shadows of our blind consumerism, that is destroying our natural environment, and of the dissociation between our actions and their deeper consequences.

Porn as a contemporary phenomenon is imbued by the collective shadow of our *hybris* and no-limits mentality.

Ulterior aspects of the male shadow, related to the personal issues of each viewer, are necessarily left aside here, as they would need the safe container of the consulting room to be fully explored.

Most of all, I decided not to deepen specific female shadow aspects related to porn in different ambits, such as: the reasons why a girl or a woman might decide to become a porn performer; the growing accessibility and enjoyment of porn videos or pictures by women; the topic of feeling betrayed by male partners when women find out they frequently enjoy porn materials. Too many times, in the history of thought, male scholars, authors, thinkers, including prominent psychoanalysts, have outlined women's way of being, their feelings, their deeper nature, and their psyche, from their unconscioulsy biased male perspective, and I would deeply regret to perpetuate this shameful patriarchal mistake, which turned very often into just another form of abuse of the feminine, as a psychic principle, and of women, as human beings. In this work, I will necessarily propose hypotheses and perspectives that concern also women, but in relation to the aspects of the feminine shadow entwined with porn, previously listed, I would prefer to engage a fruitful dialogue with women scholars, authors, and thinkers, listening to them and their feminine perspective, first.

CHAPTER SEVEN

Porn and as if

Porn can be indubitably considered an *as if* object and experience, and possesses an *as if* quality by virtue of its fictional nature.

In the early days of mass porn's popularity, sex scenes were usually inserted in the fictional frame of a movie, with costumes, roles, characters, and some sort of plot requiring some minimal acting capacities. Accordingly, many porn actors and actresses during this initial period of mass porn claimed to be considered actors and actresses as such, in all respects, only engaged in a different sector of the movie industry.

The technological development that brought the dematerialisation and the virtually infinite duplicability of internet porn has increasingly turned porn away from the movie model, and has resulted in the preparation of smaller "porn portions", ready to be consumed, more on the example of the food industry. Consequently, plots, costumes, characters, and recitation have been eclipsed, giving way to shorter, more to-the-point performances, devoid of (and disinterested in) any complex narration.

The *as if* nature of a porn scene, already evident in the early movie productions, has become the cypher of contemporary internet porn in a peculiar and contradictory way: on the one hand, the performance *per se* has been very often divested from any fictional claim, and reduced to the mere faithful record of what has factually happened, that is, the sex scene; on the other hand, the sex scene itself is performed by girls and women *as if* it were truly exciting and fulfilling for them. In other words, to the hyper-realism of the sex scene, raw and devoid of any narrative references, corresponds the deeply fictional essence of what is shown on the screen.

Especially for the actresses, in fact, porn has almost nothing to do with pleasure, albeit they are usually reluctant to admit it, in books and interviews about their work.[1] As a matter of fact, porn scenes force in particular female performers to maintain unnatural and uncomfortable postures for the sake of the shot, and their supposed pleasure has a pretty negligible space, since the actresses mostly have to withstand physical discomfort, disgust, and pain to a very high degree, as we will later outline. For this very reason, the *as if* nature of the sex scene rests solely on the shoulders of the female performers: the fictional nature of porn is preserved thanks to their hardest work, with some little cooperation by the male actors, at times; much more often, it is accomplished despite the fastidious obstacle they deliberately enact.

We will explore the implications of this dimension in the next chapter, because one of the pivotal colours of the kaleidoscope we are outlining in this work lies exactly in the fissure that separates the experiences of male and female performers in porn. The former carry out mainly the hyper-realistic side of it, often, if not always, taking pleasure from the whole process, while the latter bear the heavy burden of the *as if* quality.

Identifying themselves with the male actors, or simply enjoying the *phantom*/performance created and shot for them, in the role of voyeurs, male spectators are usually inclined to neglect the *as if* quality of porn contents, just like any spectator of any kind of movie rarely keeps in his or her mind the fictional nature of what is shown on the screen.[2] Deception is specifically sought in any film, as it actually enacts the fertile field where we can genuinely feel the emotions, be grasped by the feelings of the protagonists, identify ourselves with some of them, and relate to what is represented. Porn movies are not at all different in this regard: what is seen on the screen is considered at the same time fictional *and* true. The more the truth is left behind, so to say, the more it is possible to enjoy porn's truly fictional nature.

The concept of *as if*, moreover, appertains directly to one of the main aspects of the activity of *playing*.

In this regard, Jung aptly stated that "the creative activity of imagination frees man from his bondage to the 'nothing but' and raises him to the status of the one who plays. As Schiller says, man is completely human only when he is at play."[3]

We know from the precious work of Donald W. Winnicott how playing and creativity can be considered core elements in the process of the emerging of the ego, in a child, and fundamental experiences in adults' lives as well. Winnicott maintained that playing requires a transitional space, a third area, which is neither the internal, psychic reality, nor the outside world, although it is felt as external by the individual.[4] Playing, thus, could be considered a peculiar way to act, to treat reality in a subjective way.

In this vein, the concept of *as if* is kindred to the activity of playing, in as much as the latter implies dealing with internal contents as if they were out there, in the real world, and at the same time, treating external reality as if it were internal, subjective content.

Assuming this perspective, a common thread may connect children playing, shared playing, cultural experiences in general, artistic expressions, and even psychotherapy, because this third, potential area in which playing takes place is the area where creativity can unfold. All these human activities may be regarded as the overlapping of the potential, playing areas of two (or more) individuals.

We must not forget that playing involves *ab initio* the body, and when the potential area is conceived as the space between two people, it would naturally require mutual trust. For these reasons, sexuality rightly belongs to the activities that unfold within these overlapping playful areas.

During childhood, the discovery of one's own and of someone else's body through all the five senses may be regarded as a peculiar form of playing, entwined with the pleasure of the senses (sensuality). This activity and its vicissitudes will become part of sexual activities as soon as puberty starts and physical maturity is reached. The playful side of sexuality dwells in early forms of playing.[5]

Sex deals with the biological instinct of reproduction, as well as with socially learned ways to feel and to express desires; it deals with the experience of communion and deep intimacy, and with pleasure and passion. Often, too often, sex deals with power issues as well, with the need for dominating the other in order to acquire some sort of identity, or owning and possessing him or her. But sex can absolutely deal with playing as well, with what we previously dubbed as *pristine joy of the body*, and with the playful interaction with oneself and with the other: a ludic attitude towards the body and sexuality may turn exploring and experimenting with them into playing.

As weird as it may seem to those who condemn it *a priori*, this ludic dimension is not at all a stranger to porn. In the so-called golden age of mass porn, the 1960s and 1970s, this very dimension was often the prominent one, together with the statement of women's right to pleasure and to sexual fulfilment, as previously mentioned. A playful and joyful attitude was surely in the foreground in most of the movies of that period, but it's still possible to run into traces of the same approach scattered in current porn as well.

The viewing of porn movies and pictures, with their total openness to the body and to the wild, unhinibited sexual side of human life, may still ignite the playful elements of sexuality in the spectator, and transmit an electrical sensation of sexual readiness, both in men and women, especially when the power-related issues, the openly violent and brutal features of much of contemporary porn production, are not in clear evidence.

At the same time, we must recall that porn material can also express the very opposite to this playful, ludic dimension.

If we focus our attention on the repetitive elements, the stereotyped roles, the lack of creative fantasies, the predictable format of most of the "porn portions", and their seriality, as assembly-line products for the entertainment of isolated individuals, playing and creativity may seem quite absent, if not totally blank. In the long run, boredom can infiltrate the experience of watching this kind of porn.

The typical reaction, or antidote even, to such tedium is going for more and more extreme performances: looking for shocking images and movies becomes the easiest attempt to replace the void of creativity and of playfulness, substituting them with adrenalinic rush.

Moreover, his reduction to a mere "two senses voyeur" (sight and hearing), with his necessarily passive attitude, can result in a flattening of any sexual creativity in the spectator as well. Exactly like any other product or good of our consumerist world, porn teaches the consumer what to desire, basically turning off his own curiosity, and reducing the possibility to welcome the unexpected.

Eventually, when engaged in a real sexual intercourse, the seasoned porn spectator may realise, maybe with some uneasiness, that his approach to sex has become mostly visual: he experiences sexual intercourse *as if* he watches himself having sex with a woman: he sees the woman, her body, himself, and their interaction *as if* they were in a video.

The pleasure of sexuality may subtly slip towards its visual function, where the spectator forgets to be a real body in touch with an-other's body: such a form of disconnection from the body experience may affect the possibility of a deeper, more extended pleasure (extended to all the senses, first of all) and of being enraptured by the experience itself.

Similarly, we see many people filming or taking pictures with their own smartphones at live concerts, interposing the touchscreen between themselves and the experience of *being* at the concert, physically wrapped up by the music, to *move* and *dance* in its sonic waves, to be *enraptured* by what is going on in the present.

The perception of the concert occurs *through* the technological devices, which are able to capture images of it, fragments transformed into pixels, while the spectator is abstracted (literally drawn, pulled outside the place he or she is in) from the real ongoing experience. Immediate sharing of the pictures and the videos in social networks, stating "I am here", apparently becomes more important than to be really there, and plunge into the music. The mindset required by filming takes the spectator out of the present event, putting him or her aside of it, so to say.

Sexuality as well can become an activity that is experienced *aside*, behind the invisible screen of our vested habit to perceive the world through its images, and sex through its porn images or *phantoms*, to recall the term used by Anders for any object that is present and absent at the same time.

As previously mentioned, the porn object *per se* exists in front of us in the ambiguous, immaterial form of a picture or a scene on a screen. A physical, material object, like a magazine or a DVD, is just a *medium*, an inter-mediate way to convey another object, that is, the porn material, by definition not physically present, or more precisely, that it is present and absent at the very same time: it is present as an image or sequence of images, while it is absent, because the content of the image or sequence of images has happened elsewhere, in another space and time. In that space and time, the spectator was not present in the flesh, but in turn as a *phantom*, a sort of invisible present/absent final recipient of the action performed.

Despite its existential ambiguity, typical of every form of technologically recorded material, porn presents a field where the spectator becomes part of an interaction, that is however able to evoke embodied experiences, like any other visual object. The *phantom* of a sexual intercourse, present and absent in front of the spectator, evokes in him (or her) real excitement, lust, craving, desire, curiosity, strong emotional reactions, involvement of the senses (at least sight and hearing, as previously outlined), and eventually a real orgasm.

The virtuality of the scene interweaves with the embodied experience of the spectator, in manifold albeit different ways compared to what would happen were the spectator participating in a real sexual exchange.

However, the *as if* nature of watching porn, its virtuality, is more and more experienced as normal, since precisely we are provided with the world through its images: the experience of porn has become just one among a multitude of experiences of the same kind.

Through porn, every man is able to see literally thousands and thousands of girls and women in their sexual intimacy, to a degree and in a quantity that was simply unconceivable in any previous era. As a matter of fact, though, this occurs once again in an *as if* modality.

The spectator's excitement is surely real and embodied. The range of his emotions and sensation, partially described in the previous chapters, can be real too (from the joyful feeling of *being* an excited, sensual body, to the narcissistic nourishment deriving from the identification with dominating males abusing the weaker females, and so on). The sensation of accessing a deeper relationship with one's own sexuality, overcoming inhibitions and difficulties, can be true as well.

Still, despite having seen and having the potential to see thousands of girls and women of any age and physical appearance on demand, not a single girl or woman has been touched, smelt, tasted, caressed, licked, or penetrated in reality.

The *as if* nature of porn takes on here the colour of a powerful illusion, something unreal that has the capacity to appear as real. This illusory nature can be disturbing to realise, but the risk that this happens is apparently quite small, as our consumerist society has generally turned us into docile voyeurs, contented with surrogate experiences, disguised as fun, in several different fields.

The *as if* nature of consuming porn would become dramatically visible were the spectator to virtually move aside and watch himself as he actually is: sitting on a chair, his trousers pulled down to his knees, in front of a computer screen, alone.

From that observer position, one can painfully feel the extent to which porn does not keep the promise it makes. The excitement for the quest for the right scene and the right girl, the wandering desire, mirrored by the images or induced and taught by them, the quivering voluptousness, all the arousal is doomed to vanish, often in the very moment of the ejaculation.

Those juicy girls and women, their real flavours remain unknown, and unattainable.

The promised ocean of pleasure turns out to be just a glass of water.

But the unfulfilled and disappointed thirst will come back, the promise will renovate when desire awakes anew, the spectator will sit in front of the screen once again, ready for another portion of illusion, coveting another *as if* piece of life.

CHAPTER EIGHT

Porn and divinity

In addition to many other dimensions, the FINSEX research accurately inquired into the attitudes towards porn among the Finnish population, in three different surveys, in 1992, 1999, and 2007.[1]

In the latter survey, the statement "I find viewing pornography very arousing" was overall affirmed by eighty-two per cent of men and forty-nine per cent of women, a proportion that was noticeably higher than the results of the 1992 research, and basically in line with those found in 1999. On a closer view, among the group of young responders (eighteen to thirty-four years old), ninety per cent of men and fifty-nine per cent of women deemed porn as very arousing, while among the middle-aged responders (thirty-five to fifty-four years old), the percentage was respectively eighty-six per cent of men and fifty-seven per cent of women.

It is no surprise that porn images and videos raise the most vivid interest among men, at any age, as they primarily deal with individual, collective, and archetypal male shadows, as previously outlined, and directly address male desires, fantasies, and imagery. But it is noteworthy that young and middle-aged women's interest has been rising, especially during the 1990s, when porn colonised the internet.

The attitude regarding porn materials, according to these studies, remains markedly negative only in the older group of women responders (fifty-four to seventy-four years old). And yet, in the 2007 study, thirty-three per cent of this age group of women agreed with the statement about finding porn arousing: since it was only seventeen per cent in the 1992 research, even among this more critical group of responders, appreciation for porn almost doubled in fifteen years.

Although the major interest in porn materials seems to be still the prerogative of men, apparently women are progressively catching them up. It is nevertheless arduous to conceive some explanation for this phenomenon, because a fundamental element is missing in this kind of research: *de facto* the question of whether porn is considered very arousing does not deepen the element of *what kind* of porn the responders have in mind.

The shelves where porn products are displayed include the widest variety of genres, to a degree that is unimaginable to the inexperienced explorer. Under the label of "tender sex", for instance, one would find porn scenes that are very attentive to the cosiness and the aesthetics of the set, where men are attractive, gentle, and kind, where plenty of time is dedicated to pleasant activities for the girl or the woman, like kissing, caressing, and licking nipples, genitals, and the whole body. The emphasis in this kind of porn material is definitely on the romantic, sweet side of sexuality.

If women were thinking more of tender porn, while men had in mind the most brutal genres, this would offer quite a different perspective on those bare statistical numbers. Of course, many women can be excited by more dashing contents and harder scenes as well, possibly resonating with fantasies that they have, albeit they may not want to experience them in reality, and the same can be said about men. These and further problems in agreeing on the meaning of the word "porn" for the responders make it quite difficult to draw some clear conclusions from the mere data in this regard.

Let's be content with the rough idea that the attitude regarding porn appears to be still divided according to gender, although less so than two decades ago, and that almost the totality of young and middle-aged men show a very strong attraction for porn materials.

Reversing the perspective, according to the most recent survey in Finland, that of 2007, we can observe that sixty-seven per cent of the older group of women (fifty-four to seventy-four years old), and thirty per cent of the older group of men (again, fifty-four to seventy-four years old) did not agree with the statement about finding porn sexually very arousing. Similarly, the data for the middle-aged group (thirty-five to fifty-four years old) show that forty-three per cent of women and fourteen per cent of men do not agree with the same statement.

As silly as it may sound, these data could account for the fact that in psychoanalytical publications and books, likely written by middle-aged or older colleagues, porn is almost always depicted as negative. In fact, there is a very high probability that the academic analysis of porn phenomena lies in the hands of people who may be quite adverse to it, sometimes genuinely, sometimes only publicly, for the sake of social acceptance and respectability.[2]

Typical treatments of porn to be found in psychoanalytical works outline, for instance, its bawdy taste for details, with reference to Melanie Klein's concept of "partial objects", to emphasise the psychological immaturity of the spectator interested in such fragmented images,[3] or some porn's empty, tasteless repetitiveness is seen as an example of repetition compulsion.[4]

Porn is regarded as stripping the body (especially the feminine body) to its mere materiality and fleshliness, devoid of any deeper symbolic meaning: no secrecy, no allusions, no metaphoric referents, only the opacity of the real, and the shallowness of the raw flesh, brutally thrown to the greedy gaze of the consumers. Further, the immediate (non-mediated) access to sexual pleasure in masturbatory forms is depicted as a deteriorated shortcut to pleasure (jouissance in Lacanian terms), avoiding the prohibition and skipping the correct sequence of the oedipal plot.

To ponder on these and further critical descriptions, quite common in depth psychologies' analysis of porn, to examine them, and to refute them, if need be, exceeds the aims of the present work, as it would imply an extensive discussion of the theoretical frames and premises behind these descriptions.

Many are the colours revealing mass porn as a complex symbol of the current times, as we are trying to ascertain in these pages, and the previously sketched psychoanalytical judgements mainly stress some of its more pathological tonalities while ignoring many others.

Although valid for some individuals, it is hard to believe that this emphasis on the pathological side of the interest in porn does justice to the Finnish data we mentioned before, for instance. Is it realistic to conceive that nine men out of ten, of any age, and almost six women in ten, are sexually aroused by partial objects, are compulsively seeking for repeated patterns, are excited by the objectification and depersonalisation of someone involved in sexual acts, devoid of any symbolic meaning and narrative, or are fixated to pre-oedipal stages, looking for an easy enjoyment, in defiance of the law of the reality principle?

I would maintain, instead, that a deeper reflection on the question of what is felt as so powerfully exciting and arousing in watching porn images and videos, especially from the perspective of men, is needed. Interestingly enough, in the broad debate about the topic of mass porn in the last thirty years, attempts to address this question directly are quite rare.

It is clearly a daunting task to speculate on the motivations that may bring a boy or a man to feel powerfully attracted to porn, as there may be several of them, overlapping and merging with each other, some individual and personal, some cultural and collective, some conscious and some unconscious. Nevertheless, a hypothesis about these motivations may open up broader meaning, and further possibilities to comprehend porn as a complex symbol of our current era.

In his *Di(zion)ario erotico* (2000), the Italian writer and journalist Massimo Fini, referring to George Bataille, maintains that the essence of eroticism is "profanation". According to his view, sexuality would allow men to degrade a woman (in the multiple meaning of "declassing", "downgrading", "debasing", "abasing") to her animal, female nature. Hence, a woman would be stripped of her social identity, status, and personal features, and the "female" element would emerge in its brightest degree. The most exciting aspect here, in Fini's opinion, would be woman's capitulation: porn, as such, would visually illustrate both the profanation and the capitulation of women.[5]

Albeit slightly tempered by the statement that, degraded to a female, a woman would be brought back to her deepest value, that is, to be in a much closer contact with nature and with herself than could be possible for a man, this perspective seems to me obscured by a thick patriarchal halo.

The strong accent on the idea of "degradation", the hinted pleasure in the actions of abasement and downgrading, highly resonate with that shadow aspect, mentioned in Chapter Six, typical of the psychologically weak patriarchal man, trying to obtain some surrogate identity through the use and the abuse of power over someone else. Certainly, degradation and abasement are some of the most visible colours of contemporary mass porn, as outlined in that chapter, but they appear to me insufficient to account for the fascination of porn for the majority of men.[6]

Leaving aside all the various individual motivations, impossible to detect and summarise, I would suggest that men essentially find very exciting girls and women *willing to do anything*, or *willing to let someone do anything* to them.

From the perspective of the woman performer (a point of view that is often deplorably forgotten in the literature on porn), this *anything* results in them moving along a *spectrum* of actions oriented towards a pole that I would dub the *non-differentiated*. In the context of a porn scene, a gradual progression towards the *non-differentiated* is the cypher of women's performances.

As a matter of fact, a girl or a woman basically performs actions that stand out for their being progressively more difficult and demanding, as they imply the management (and possibly the control) of sensations and emotions belonging to the fields of discomfort, vexation, disgust, and pain. In other words, a skip, a *displacement* is requested of women performers: they have to abolish the differentiation between what is felt to be good and what is felt to be bad, and they have to act *as if* everything they experience were wondrous, exciting, yearned for, and coveted.

The differentiation between what is pleasant and what is unsavoury, what is enjoyable and what is disgusting, what is amusing and what is painful, is progressively subsumed, as the female performer proceeds on the *spectrum* towards the polarity of the *non-differentiated*. It is possible to find every single step on this *continuum* on the internet, from the less demanding actions to the most extreme ones, and from complete successes to failed attempts.

A girl or a woman steps forward, on such a *spectrum*, in the very moment she strips off, and exposes herself in front of the camera eye. Even taking into account the possible pleasure from self-exhibition, and the current need for visibility as a substitute for our uncertain, liquid identities, as outlined in Chapter Five, we can imagine some degree of more or less conscious discomfort for a woman in consigning her intimacy, her nakedness, the most private images of her body (the foundation of who we are) in its bare vulnerability, to an impersonal, amoral, eventually uncontrollable container, as the internet is. In that inceptive moment, she basically surrenders to becoming virtually visible on demand, possibly to millions of invisible eyes.

The idea of our image left forever in the hands of a virtual container, available to everyone surfing on porn sites, shared, linked, saved, forwarded, used, totally outside our control (and surely with a miserable profit in return, compared to the price paid), could be nightmarish, were we keeping it in mind.

I have very serious doubts, for instance, that a girl could do anything in order to withdraw her porn images and videos, were she to change her mind at a future time about having allowed herself to be transformed into a public product for all eternity. Letting her own image been taken away from her and used is an action that could evoke profound uneasiness. But this is only the initial step on the *spectrum* we are sketching here, and probably the least evident for the performers themselves.

The uneasiness, for a female performer, is likely to increase in relation to letting someone (who is often unknown, rarely attentive, and usually unpleasant) physically enter inside her, penetrating every orifice she has.[7]

The effort to *displace* negative emotions into a positive "place", that is, polarity, thence, occurs from the very start of the scene-shooting. Internet porn can actually be seen as an extremely detailed compendium of girls and women gradually approaching the *non-differentiated*.

Unlike in the earlier days of porn, when the final product was almost always presenting the successful abolition of differences, so that the skip/displacement process went almost unnoticed, contemporary voyeurs of internet porn have full access to all the degrees of this highly demanding path.

The no-limits mentality and the consequent tendency to extreme of porn performances, sketched in Chapter Five, perfectly match the unabashed movement towards the highest degrees on the *continuum*. Casting videos, scenes shot outside the old professional porn movie industry, thematic sites featuring beginner porn-girls,[8] and the unlimited access to anything that can be uploaded by non-professionals or amateurs, have created a complex "pornscape" where anyone can easily find all the tinges of the challenging and not infrequently painful attempts to tend towards the *non-differentiated*, performed by the actresses.

Pivotal elements for a successful attempt to reach positions on the *spectrum* that are closer and closer to the pole of *non-differentiation* are the woman's face, her gaze and her eyes. Facial expressions in general, together with moaning of pleasure, are absolutely essential to this achievement.

This is the reason why porn scenes that monotonously focus on close-ups of the mere genitals, for minutes and minutes, are very boring to the majority, and are rated negatively by spectators themselves: good porn, in fact, needs this approach towards the *non-differentiated* to be clearly in evidence.

The actress' face is *the* place where the abolition of differences between good and bad, and the representation of the action *as if* it were pleasant, amusing, and wonderful, can be fully embodied and shown: as Regazzoni concisely puts it, "The female face is the heart, the centre, the core of porn" (2010, p. 133; translated for this edition).

By contrast, men's faces tend to be more and more marginal, or even absent, in current mass porn. Whichever facial expressions they may assume during the sexual performance are pretty useless, if not disturbing, for the spectator who (unconsciously, *nota bene*) enjoys the view of the women's progress on the *spectrum*. A significant change from the early days of porn, when male performers' faces were mandatorily filmed right before or while reaching orgasm, to the contemporary one, lies exactly in the progressive eclipsing of men's faces.

The centre of the scene is the realm of girls and women, of their faces and their juicy bodies, while men are more and more reduced to a "pubic presence", so to say, framed as they are from the belly to half of the thigh. Men's requirements are just an enduring, good-enough erection, possibly a big penis, useful for the necessary shooting perspectives, and a final ejaculation, or better, cumshot.

A substantial exception to this eclipse is when the man's face is needed in order to accentuate the actress' process towards the *non-differentiated*: when male performers are particularly unsightly, hideous, old, or all of these together, for example, the process becomes even more noticeable.[9] Generally speaking, though, showing men's faces has become basically unnecessary.

The *continuum*, thus, is a scale of increasingly discomforting, disgusting, and even painful actions, performed *as if* they were extremely pleasant by the female performers: the skip exactly resides in this displacement of feelings, from their right "place" to a fictional one of pleasure. Towards the pole of *non-differentiation* the actress reaches what I would dub the "equivalence of all her holes", as well as the "equivalence of all the body fluids".[10]

By virtue of the extremity of performances, perfectly fitting the no-limits frame our Western world inhabits, girls and women in porn very often take giant steps on the *spectrum* we are sketching here, to a degree that is hardly possible to reach for women who are not in porn.[11]

The internet displays every step, from the first, difficult, and often failed attempts to tolerate and control discomfort, disgust, or pain, to almost complete successes, where the *non-differentiation* is accomplished to a very high grade, and where the *as if*, fictional pleasure is performed masterfully.

Male performers, in contrast, are not required to effect any sort of *displacement*: what they perform is often, if not always, a source of real pleasure, something liked by them in reality, and supposedly by almost any other man to be enjoyable, were he in their place. This is the reason why I previously maintained that no real transgression is actually enacted by men in porn:[12] their performances are always the same, absolutely predictable, and within the comfortable limits of what they indeed like: the weight of trespassing limits, and most of all, the *displacement* needed in order to progress towards the *non-differentiated* solely rests on women's shoulders.

This perspective may feed the aversion and abhorrence towards porn materials of those who already are deeply critical of them: the clear imbalance between what is required of men and of women in porn, the hardest labour falling to the latter, the concept itself of advancing towards a polarity of *non-differentiation*, may all be connected to those ideas of degradation, profanation, and abasement of the feminine previously mentioned.

But speaking of the *non-differentiated*, we truly enter a territory which would probably be considered the most distant from that of porn.

Human consciousness unfolds and expresses itself in the *difference*, in the distinctions that avoid the con-fusion of things. Proceeding towards the *non-differentiated*, thus, would correspond to a gradual abandonment of conscious subjectivity, and to a movement towards the indistinct background that preceeds the birth of consciousness itself.

Human beings have always placed the indistinct and the *non-differentiated* beyond what is human, in the realm of the sacred and the divine.[13] The indistinct, that is, the background from which consciousness emerges over the history of millennia, has been usually perceived as the original chaos from which human beings needed to differentiate, and that they always feared.

Rudolf Otto, in his book entitled *The Sacred* (1917), analysed the mode of religious experience, and defined the feeling of human beings in the presence of the divine and the sacred as the *numinous* (from the Latin *numen*, god). Facing the radical other (*ganz andere*, in German), the *mysterium tremendum* of a potency beyond the human and the natural world, a mixture of fascination and revulsion, a powerful attraction mixed with an unsettling feeling of dread, emerge. Numinosity implies exactly this combination of fascination and terror, perceived at the presence of the sacred, in whatever form it may be embodied.

As Mircea Eliade underlines, "When the sacred manifests itself, any object becomes *something else*, without ceasing to be *itself* [...] A *sacred* stone remains a stone; ostensibly (or more exactly: from a profane perspective) nothing distinguishes it from all the other stones" (Eliade, 2006, p. 15; translated for this edition).

In other words, in the realm of the sacred and the divine, a thing or an object can be at the same time another thing, in open contrast to Aristotle's principle of non-contradiction, moving towards the state of *non-differentiation*.

Maintaining that the *non-differentiated* has always been placed in the realm of the sacred suggests the reflection that when women in porn move on the *spectrum* towards the polarity of *non-differentiation*, they evoke something that in previous eras of the human history of consciousness would have been perceived contiguous to the divine.

The numinous quality and the sacral significance of sexuality itself have been explored and described by several authors, whose work draws together the deep connections between sex and religion or spirituality.[14] The history of religions shows these evident connections, for example in Hindu tantric rituals, in the rich mythological material reaching us from the Mesopotamian area, and in the Mediterranean cultures and cults of antiquity, especially in Egypt, Greece, and Rome. Despite the blatant disregard for the body and for sexuality imposed by Judaism and Christianity throughout the history of Western culture, traces of these connections can be found scattered within their stories, traditions, and sacred texts as well,[15] while they are more clearly visible in Gnosticism.

C. G. Jung has acknowledged the tight relation between religion and sexuality, underlining the close association between the sexual instinct and the striving for wholeness, which is part of what he called the religious instinct of the psyche.

During the summer of 1993, in Avignon, France, James Hillman gave a talk entitled *Pink Madness*, an expression he used to describe erotic imagery in porn. Three years later, Bobbie Yow, the manager of the C. G. Jung Bookstore of Los Angeles, gave voice to her own "frustration at Hillman's cavalier view of pornography and his conclusion regarding its value", in an article.[16]

Hillman's premise was that the erotic imagination has to be unfettered in order to allow the process of differentiation of our instincts and their transformation: for the sake of this precious goal, in his opinion, the erotic imagination, visible in porn, should be allowed total freedom and right of expression. He also added that "the attack on pornography is aimed at the exculpation of imagination at its instinctual roots. The attack on pornography is a continuation of the attack on the pagan gods and on the body of Aphrodite."[17]

Coherent to his theoretical approach, Hillman appointed the ancient Greek gods and goddesses as the archetypal elements behind our unconscious psychic functioning: porn, in his opinion, would be in the realm of the ancient Greek goddess of love, Aphrodite, and, at the same time, would serve the minor god (and Aphrodite's son) Priapus.

The mythical sources chosen by Hillman, and followed by the author of the article, Yow, acknowledge Priapus as the son of Aphrodite and Zeus. Accordingly, Hillman reckoned Hera, Zeus' notoriously jealous wife, as the archetypal element responsible for the definitions of porn as detrimental: as archetype of wives and mothers, Hera would embody the denigration of porn, because of her hateful denial of Priapus' right to exist.

Although agreeing on the reference to Priapus, in her article Yow is highly critical of Hillman's point of view. In her own words, she finds it very

> difficult to situate Aphrodite as the primary archetypal energy behind pornography. It seems more likely that pornography, particularly hard-core pornography, is completely lacking in Aphrodite and Eros energy. As concretised and rigidified erotic imagination at its most primitive level, it seems to me that pornography comes more under the auspices of Chronos than Aphrodite.[18]

A few paragraphs before this, Yow expresses her contempt for porn, considered as "repetitively boring, empty of story line, or primitively simplistic, indicative of a disconnection from the feminine to serve its own ends". Again, she maintains that "[pornographic] fantasy seldom moves beyond sterile repetition-compulsion".

I report in detail this critical point of view on porn, as it is an appropriate example of the typical psychoanalytical perspective, emphasising only its negative colours, so to say: repetitive, boring, empty, primitive, with no imagination, addictive.[19]

As painful as it can be for a Jungian scholar or analyst, these very adjectives could be used by a rationalist to describe religious rituals as well. A ritual is by definition repetitive, as it requires a precise sequence of actions that have to be followed with the utmost care. A ritual can be seen as a primitive way to deal with projected unconscious contents by a less differentiated psyche. The profound need for a community to iterate the ritual again and again may be seen as addictive, in the wider meaning of a needed and constant repetition and renewal of the ritual, in order to avoid a growing feeling of anguish. Most likely, from the perspective of a rational mentality, the whole process of a ritual would be described as empty, meaningless, and quite boring as such.

In her agreement on the reference to Priapus, besides, Yow's statements and inferences are apparently based only on one of many versions of the myth. Depending on the sources, in fact, Priapus is actually given four different fathers: Zeus (as Hillman and Yow choose to endorse), Dionysus, Hermes, or Adonis. This minor god appears to be a much more complex figure than we may think: including other mythical sources, his complexity increases dramatically, inviting us to more cautious, nuanced interpretations on his deeper meaning, as should always be the case, with symbols and dreams as well. If a myth is a collective dream of a community or a culture, as Jungians we should always be careful and avoid rigid or narrow interpretations.

Yow's statement that porn reflects the complete absence of Aphrodite is particularly striking. Apparently, she acknowledges her presence only in eroticism.[20] By doing so, she pursues a quite common view that differentiates eroticism clearly from porn, the former being the good, deep, symbolic one, while the latter is the bad, flat, vulgar one.

Actually, women in porn unconsciously embody most of the postures and gestures in which Aphrodite herself has traditionally been portrayed in classical iconography (statues, paintings), as well as her depiction in myths: porn actresses inadvertently enter the goddess of love's realm in the very moment they undress and expose their naked bodies. In the original statues of Aphrodite from ancient Greece, or in their masterful reproductions from the Roman era, she often "appears preparing for a bath, loosening a sandal, placing her hands over her breasts and pubic area, glancing back over her shoulder to see her buttocks, or tending to her bracelets and other adornments. She seems to enjoy looking at herself and being looked at" (Moore, 1999, pp. 20–21).

Aphrodite, her enchanting body naked, allures, tempts, and charms the onlookers even nowadays, often wearing a mischievous smile: one of her many epithets, in fact, was *philommeides*, meaning "loving of laughters and smiles", but also the very similar *philommedes*, "genital-loving", according, for instance, to Hesiod.[21] Aphrodite could be called *parakyptousa*, "watching from a window", glancing at the onlooker always indirectly, and *kataskopia*, peeping, spying. She was sometimes identified as *Peitho*, that is, persuasion, seduction, and even as *Porne*, prostitute, hinting at the very core of our reflections.

Porn actresses, modern "lovers of the genitals", undress and expose their apparently juicy, tasty bodies, while maliciously smiling and artfully peeping sidelong, towards the invisible spectators, in an open gesture of seduction, communicated especially through their wondrous gaze.

Anasyrma is another very interesting appellation of the goddess of love and beauty, where *ana* is the ancient Greek for "up", "back", and *syrma* means "skirt". The Greek word indicates the "exposing of the genitals" by a woman, and plainly refers to the numinous quality of the feminine genitals, as this was experienced in several ancient religious rituals and dances belonging to different cultures and cults. In ancient Greece, for instance, the gesture of *anasyrma* was not the prerogative of Aphrodite, but it was fully part of the cults of Dionysus, Demeter, and Persephone as well.

The numinous potency of this olden gesture is still very present in current porn, and it should be noted that before the beginning of mass porn, short movies produced since the early 1960s (sometimes eloquently called "spread") showed a girl or a woman undressing, gradually unveiling her body and her genitals, until she remained naked and spread her pussy, with the brightest, radiant smile.

Again, Aphrodite was called *kallipygos*, that is, "characterised by beautiful buttocks": the posture of Aphrodite *kallipygos* may be considered another variant of *anaysrma*, where the goddess of grace and desire exposes her backside and her beautiful, attractive ass, while artfully peeping over her shoulder. It is needless to say how this kind of posture is abundantly present in current porn, either performed alone, while stripping, or during sexual intercourse, when the actresses are taken from behind, moaning and gazing over their shoulders, like Aphrodite, to the camera's eyes, to the spectator.

Thomas Moore claims that "*anasyrma* may be surrounded by taboo, fascination and ritual, but these are all signs of the shadow side of the sacred" (Moore, 1999, p. 57).

This reference to the shadow side of the sacred allows us to mention that, according to other mythical sources, Aphrodite had dark sides as well: beyond being the goddess of love, grace, beauty, desire, and sex, she contained within herself a multiplicity of aspects, probably inherited from other similar goddesses from which her cult derived, like the ancient Akkadian Ishtar (Astarte, in Hellenised form; Ashtoreth for the Hebrews), who was linked with sexuality, fertility, love, but also with war and power, and her more ancient Sumerian counterpart, Inanna. In reference to this lesser known, darker side of Aphrodite, Kerényi recounts further appellations like *melainis*, "the black"; *scotia*, "the obscure"; *anosia*, "the impious"; and also more unsettling epithets like *androphonos*, "the burier of men", or *tymborichos*, generally "the burier". Again, as *epitymbia*, she appeared like "the one who sits on the graves".[22]

All these interesting references remind us that it would be quite partial to inclose the presence of Aphrodite only in eroticism, supposedly considered a more positive, creative, and soulful activity than the vulgar porn. This goddess indeed possessed a manifold personality, and complex cross-references to shadowy, destructive sides as well, to the point that she was sometimes counted among the Furies. Porn possibly shows the presence of Aphrodite exactly as eroticism, or even more, since porn can easily resonate with the darker elements of this goddess, who is related in complex ways to passion, desire, sexuality, creativity, life, but also to power, destructiveness, and death, like the ancient goddesses of the Mesopotamian area from which she descends.

At any rate, the significance that could be drawn out from the exchange between Hillman and Yow, beyond their divergent interpretation about which gods or archetypal elements may be shaping hardcore materials, is that they both implicitly agree on the numinous nature of porn. This is what matters most to our reflections: porn can be felt as numinous, as sexuality has always been considered in the history of religions, and this numinosity may account for the powerful fascination of the majority of men for it, much more than pathological motives.

Girls and women in porn often shine with a sort of radiant numinosity, *in primis* from their naked bodies, from their faces, and from their enchanting glances.

I would maintain that this does not happen only because in their gestures they relive the eternal gestures of Aphrodite herself, or those of other goddesses of love, or because supposed archetypal elements would unconsciously resonate in hard-core scenes, but because sexuality itself has traditionally been a form of gnosis and sacred ritual for millennia, and most of all, because of the previously outlined movement of the female performers on the *spectrum* towards the *non-differentiated*.

This latter is the phenomenon that would transpose current mass porn into a territory that, in previous eras, would have rightly pertained to the sacred and the divine. The movement toward the *non-differentiated* enacted by girls and women in porn is an expression of the startling power of the feminine to embody the divine, and it transforms female performers into what, in former phases of the history of consciousness, would have been called "goddesses" or at least "goddess' priestesses".

My hypothesis is that the widespread fascination for porn may represent a sort of unconscious nostalgia for the sacred and the divine in an epoch like ours when all the previous frames of meaning (mythological, religious, metaphysical) have waned, and when the gap between the "death of god", on a collective level, and the acute need of meaning, on the individual level, becomes painfully felt, albeit not clearly acknowledged on a conscious plane.

CHAPTER NINE

Porn and lost goddesses

> Naked, every woman embodies Nature, *prakrti*. We should contemplate her with the same admiration and the same detachment that we reserve for regarding the impenetrable mystery of Nature […] If, before the woman in her nudity, we cannot perceive in our own intimate core that same terrifying emotion that one feels before the revelation of a mystery, there is no rite—there is only a profane act.
>
> —*Eliade*, 2015, p. 9; translated for this edition

In the words of Mircea Eliade, the renowned historian of religions, Hindu awareness of the contiguity of the feminine with the sacred and the divine resonates with all its clarity.

In the same essay on the erotic Indian mystic, Eliade mentions the story of the wise Vasistha, who went to query Buddha about the rites in honour of the goddess Tara. Great was his incredulity when he noticed that Buddha was surrounded by thousands of female lovers, in mystical ecstasy. As he got closer to him, Buddha whispered in his ear: "Women are gods, women are life, women are the adornment. Be always among them, with your mind" (Eliade, 2015, pp. 13–14; translated for this edition).

Beyond their nudity, holy and numinous in itself, beyond their postures, their glances, their smiles, all resonating with the gestures traditionally attributed to female goddesses related to love, beauty, desire, and sexuality, girls and women in porn would gradually (and unwittingly) enter the realm of the sacred, approaching *non-differentiation*, through their movement on a *spectrum* of difficult actions, performed *as if* they were enjoyed to the utmost.

The outcome of this process could be dubbed as "intimation of hierophany" (that is, an allusion to an apparition of the sacred), and would mark a radical difference between the feminine and the masculine: in fact, a similar process performed by a male actor would not obtain the same outcome, not even remotely, at least in heterosexual porn. Enacting the previously outlined *displacement*, and moving towards the polarity of *non-differentiation*, a male performer would most probably seem not at all exciting, if not disgusting, for a woman spectator, and would hardly be perceived as contiguous to the sacred and the divine.[1]

Under this particular perspective, the famous statement by Emmanuel Levinas about "the exceptional position of the feminine in the economy of being" may come to our minds.

As Jungians, though, we are well aware of the coexistence of feminine and masculine elements within the psyche of both men and women. This implies that, when we speak of the feminine, we do not intend women as such, rather a psychological principle, present in the male psyche as well.

Still, in relation with the ability to move towards the *non-differentiated*, a radical difference between women and men seems to emerge, as the power of the feminine to embody certain qualities of the divine and the sacred appears to be much broader and deeper than that of the masculine.[2]

The unconscious perception by males of this immense power could account for the deliberate devaluation, the intentional abasement, and the open disparagement often enacted by men in porn against female performers: albeit being direct witnesses of their exertion to displace discomfort, disgust, and pain in the opposite polarity, acting *as if* their experience were unimaginably pleasurable, men apparently make the process much more difficult on purpose, and hinder it, even, often veering towards more abusive and brutal behaviours.

The already challenging attempt to ride the wave of the elusive, constantly moving point of the *as if*, always on the verge of its subsidence, so to say, is often boycotted, and doomed to fail by male performers' inattentiveness or deliberate sabotage. The effort of performing extreme actions *as if* they were pleasant, thus, runs the serious risk of collapsing, and women's numinous smiles, glances, and moaning, easily cross the very thin line that separates them from the countenance of discomfort and barely controlled pain.

The most extreme examples of current porn scenes not rarely show the failure of female performers to accomplish the *displacement* we have previously described, at the hands of men who enact the parody of the patriarchal idiot, apparently behaving as if what they do would be what "those sluts" indeed like, and surely deserve.

It is not impossible to detect here a significant example of "envy of the vagina", were we to believe in such a concept. Or better, this could be considered a clear example of an ill-concealed envy of the uncontainable power of the feminine, and of its greater contiguity to the sacred.

Nevertheless, despite the attempts to abase and humiliate them, and even when apparently succumbing under the burden of these diminishing behaviours, female performers keep standing in the very centre of the scene, with their radiancy and their potency preserved, the sole reason of the existence of the scene itself, the sole source of its beauty. The discrepancy between their bright numinosity and the futile staging of the patriarchal antics only increases.[3]

Reportedly, the annoyance of female actresses for the boycotting behaviours enacted by their male partners is quite conspicuous, as it sometimes emerges in their autobiographical testimonies.[4] This fact could explain why more and more scenes in the pornscape show girls and women acting all kinds of lesbian performances (in most cases not being even bisexual), reaching as extreme peaks as those shot with male actors, but avoiding their undesirable presence.

Men's pointlessness seems to reach its apex in the so-called "fucking machine" genre, where in fact a machine substitutes male performers in their essential role of penetrating and enduring.[5] After all, the male role in the progress towards the *non-differentiated* is to some extent subsidiary, and it can be consequently enacted by reliable mechanical substitutes. The essence of women's performances in porn remains the same, with or without men: that is, a gradual movement towards the *non-differentiated*, and thus the divine.

As previously intimated, my hypothesis is that the unconscious motivation to be at the same time unsettled, attracted, and fascinated by porn materials is a deep feeling of nostalgia for what, in ancient times, would have been called "the sacred".

Contemporary porn could be seen as the desacralised, technological, and consumerist counterpart of the so-called "sacred prostitution", a ritual institution in the honour of Inanna, the Sumerian goddess of love, passion, fertility, and warfare, as portrayed by Nancy Qualls-Corbett in a book of hers.[6] Inanna was a moon goddess, afterwards worshipped as Ishtar in Babylonia, as Anahita by the Persians, and as Anath, Astarte, or Ashtart by the Canaanites and the Phoenicians. In Egypt, she was originally called Hathor, and later on Isis. The same type of goddess was known as Cybele in Lydia, Aphrodite in Greece, and Venus in ancient Rome.

The sacred prostitute was a woman devoted to Inanna, who served in her temple: "Her beauty, her graceful movements, her freedom from ambivalence, anxieties or self-consciousness towards her sexuality, all attributes of the goddess as well, derive from the reverence she holds for her feminine nature" (Qualls-Corbett, 1988, p. 68).

The following physical description of the sacred prostitute may perfectly fit most of the girls or women in current porn as well: "Her gestures, her facial expressions and movement of her supple body all speak to the welcoming of passion [...] Her movements are graceful, as she is well aware of her beauty [...] in her ecstasy she forgets all restraints and gives herself to [...] the stranger" (Qualls-Corbett, 1988, p. 22).

The sacred prostitute was supposed to welcome and to have sexual intercourse, after appropriate rituals, with a stranger, considered to be the emissary of the gods, who had come to Inanna's temple to worship the goddess of love. Hence, their sexual exchange was consecrated to the goddess herself, and led to the transformation of both the protagonists of the ritual.

Religion and sexuality, in these kinds of rituals, were deeply intertwined, as was often the case in Eastern religions' traditions: "Desire and sexual response experienced as a regenerative power were recognised as a gift or a blessing from the divine. Man's and woman's sexual nature and their religious attitude were inseparable [...] they offered the sex act to the goddess revered for love and passion" (Qualls-Corbett, 1988, pp. 30–31).

Sacred prostitution devoted to the different goddesses of love, sex, and fertility went on for thousands of years, inside different cultures, in relation to fertility rites aimed at propitiating abundant harvests, at the initiation of girls and brides into womanhood, or when there was the need of revelations from the goddess.

The sacred prostitutes were adored and worshipped as the goddess herself, and accordingly enjoyed various privileges and a peculiar status in the society of their times, unlike the profane prostitutes, who were despised, abused, abased, and cast out.

The frames of meaning of that ancient world where sacred prostitution had a precise place and important ritual functions have been buried under more than four millennia of human history.

The advent of patriarchy, the transition from polytheism to Judaic and Christian monotheisms, the split between matter and spirit, the repression of the body and the feminine, the consequent demonisation of sexuality, the gradual fading of any mythological, religious, and metaphysical frames, and the epochal rupture of the "death of God", are some of the milestones that we can quickly mention, and that have led to our current technological, desacralised, disenchanted world.

Lovemaking is obviously no more a ritual to call upon the goddess of sex and love, as sexuality as such is no more honoured as a form of holy knowing. Residual, surviving rites may just resemble pale vestiges of what they had represented in previous eras, as our whole way-of-being-in-the-world has become essentially profane.

According to Mircea Eliade, though, "the majority of the non religious people still behave religiously, although unawarely […] Modern men, who pretends to feel and to be irreligious, have at their disposal a camouflaged mythology, and several degraded rituals" (Eliade, 2006, p. 129; translated for this edition). Eliade avers that "the *profane* is nothing but a new manifestation of the same constitutive structure of human beings, that previously was manifested through sacred expressions" (ibid., p. 10; translated for this edition).

Under this perspective, porn as well may hold some of the elements that in very ancient eras had been related to the sacred and the divine, but manifested and displayed in degraded forms, since we live in a totally different moment of the history of consciousness: *de facto* we are "metaphysically naked", outside any mythical and religious container, in a technological world where everything functions but does not offer sense/direction, in relation to the ultimate meaning of life.[7]

This "metaphysical nakedness" is unconsciously perceived by the large majority of post-modern human beings, as a background anguish with no name, and could account for an equally unconscious nostalgia for those lost containers that used to confer meaning in previous eras.

Among the many colours we have tried to illustrate in the present work, porn could be considered also as the vestige of ancient rituals, performed in the total absence of the frames that used to contain them and give them individual and collective meaning, and transformed into a technological mass product instead.

This specific colour may bring to mind Luigi Zoja's reflections in an interesting work of his, about drug addiction.[8] Zoja avers that behind the growing consumption of drugs and alcohol in Western societies of the last forty years, it is possible to see a powerful, unconscious need of initiation. In his work, the ancient sacrality of initiation rites is placed in relation to the destructive forms it assumes in the current materialistic and consumerist world.

It is once again Mircea Eliade who reminds us that the biggest difference between archaic societies and the contemporary world lies in the disappearance of initiation, and of its rites of passage. Our current desacralised, technological, and consumerist world is very likely to produce a deep feeling of meaninglessness in its inhabitants, hence an equally intense need of change, renewal, and transformation, aimed at regaining the lost meaning and a more rooted sense of identity.

In ancient societies, initiation was exactly complying these deep needs for change, renewal, and transformation, and implied different rites of passage. These rites were essentially expressing an initiatic death, and a subsequent initiatic rebirth.

The eclipse of initiation, and most of all, of the mythical, religious, and ultimately metaphysical frames in which initiation had a meaning may increase an unconscious expectation of renewal, transformation, and meaning to the utmost, in a world that however does not offer them any more.

Zoja's hypothesis is that the abuse of drugs and alcohol could be seen as a failed attempt to regain some form of initiation, aimed at the possible transformation of lives that are felt as miserable and meaningless. Apparently, in these contemporary attempts, the phase of the initiatic rebirth is accessed directly, skipping the fundamental step of the initiatic death. Moreover, everything happens outside the traditional containers that used to exist and protect the initiate: for instance, taking drugs under the control of the wise old members of the tribe, sharing the experience with others, following precise steps that included waivers, obligations, and so on.

In a world dominated by the no-limits mentality, as outlined in Chapter Five, the initiatic hope can easily degenerate in an uncontrolled, compulsive consumption of drugs or alcohol, and turn into an addiction, furthermore accomplishing the implicit goal pursued by our consumerist model, as previously illustrated. Such degeneration marks the failure of any initiation, whose need is in turn doomed to increase, and result in alternative means of satisfaction.

This need of a deep renewal and transformation is mostly unconscious, we said. In order to really make it happen, we should first of all become aware of it, and consciously face the terrible lack of means to access it offered by our current world. A rebellion to the coordinates and the ingredients of our technological, consumerist society appears to be the precondition of what Jung dubbed "individuation process", as it could be intended by the post-modern human being.[9]

Drawing a parallel to Zoja's hypothesis about drug addiction, I reckon that a similar nostalgia for the sacred could powerfully account for the widespread attraction to porn imagery and its numinous fascination. In the field of porn as well, the slip towards a repetitive, compulsive consumption, and towards addiction, may be considered as the degeneration of the original unconscious need into the typical surrogate, simplified forms offered by consumerism.

It is now possible to understand the manifold meaning of the title of this work, which is the title of this chapter as well: the goddesses are lost, firstly because the whole frame of sacrality that used to contain them has been lost as well, a long time ago.

The numinosity of the feminine, the holiness of the body and of sexuality itself, have become barely visible, almost neglected, because the container that bestowed meaning on them has vanished, and what used to be connected to a ritual has now become a mere product. As such, the ritual has turned into a degraded parody of what it used to be, and has gained the characteristic (actually very valuable, from the point of view of consumerism) of hinting at something ultimately unattainable.

The vanishing of any previous container leaves space to a burning nostalgia for the sacred that feeds the fascination for its allusions, and this happens in porn as well: as vestiges of what once was sacred, porn *de facto* promises an impossible fulfilment for a need that is unconscious, and that, for this very reason, is extremely powerful.

But the goddesses are indeed lost.

We cannot simply go back to the previous forms of containment and re-build the frames of meaning that used to confer direction to our lives; rather, we should look at the whole need of the sacred from a very different, more adult perspective.[10] But these reflections would open up the deeply complex topic of how to compound the gap between the human need of frames of meaning, still present, and the current phase of the history of consciousness, essentially frameless, godless, and desacralised, a topic that far exceeds the aim of these pages.

Going back to the title of this book, it is possible to illustrate further ways in which we can state that the goddesses are lost: from the perspective of girls and women in porn, for instance, their very relationship with their own divinity and sacrality is often lost too. In most cases, female performers do not seem to realise their own powerful numinosity and their contiguity to the sacred when they move on the *spectrum* towards the *non-differentiated*. Furthermore, their working environment, especially their male partners on the set, do not even remotely help them to achieve this acknowledgement, rather they substantiate their devaluation. Lastly, their sacrality and numinosity are usually denied by most of the women who are not in porn, as well as by the radical anti-porn feminists, who actually harshly criticise their choice to let men exploit, use, and abuse them and their bodies.

As for counterbalancing this general diminishing attitude towards them, some actresses can run the risk of falling towards the opposite polarity, becoming inflated by their possible divinity, so to say. Some form of *hybris* can possess them, in the process of approaching the *non-differentiated*, and facilitate the achievement of tremendous degrees of extreme, with a worrying denial of limits that would be reasonable to respect, for their own physical and psychological safety.[11]

On the male spectator's side, instead, we may find a profound ambivalence towards the numinosity and sacrality of female actresses.

On the one hand, men of any age who show the strongest attraction for girls and women in porn reveal that the ancient worship of the goddesses of love can still survive, disguised in other forms of fascination. Men, for instance, can become devoted fans and admirers of this or that girl or woman star: they may faithfully buy her movies, they positively rate her videos, and express their devotion in the comments at the bottom of the web pages where these videos are uploaded; they may even crave to know the names of unknown girls they come across, in order to look for further material performed by them, and to follow them, with admiration and gratitude, even.[12]

On the other hand, though, the typical patriarchal hypocrisy may emerge, with its set of devaluing epithets towards what is actually strongly desired and coveted: names like "dirty bitch", "whore", "slut", go hand in hand with an attitude of denial for their subjectivity, as men rarely acknowledge women's painful efforts to move towards the *non-differentiated*, that is, their subjective experience. How women really feel before, throughout, and after the whole performance is not the male spectator's business, in honour of the commandment to do only one's own job, and to ignore the consequences of one's own actions, as explained in Chapter Four.

Men's acknowledgement of the numinosity of porn women's sexuality is destined to collapse miserably in the inconvenient case their female partners would embody it in their own lives. The patriarchal double morality emerges in all its force, in the forms of harsh blame, and even violent condemnation, of the same behaviours that would turn porn actresses into numinous goddesses. Admiration can be subtended just if the "bitch" is someone else, not their wife or girlfriend, and this shows the weak root of the idea of women's sexual numinosity as a value in itself.

The ambivalence we are outlining here concerns porn actresses as well, however: together with admiration, lust, gratitude, and desire, men can feel open contempt and devaluation, similar to what happened to the profane prostitute in ancient Greece, who was usually dismissed as a subject, used and abused at will as an object.

Millennia of evolution of the spirit appear to have been useless, here as well as in many other human behaviours and habits.

Again, the title speaking of "lost goddesses" could refer to the (often ignored, if not completely neglected) subjective experience of the female porn performers as well. In the challenging effort of reaching deeper levels of *non-differentiation*, girls and women in porn progressively lose their own subjectivity, and move towards the transpersonal, or impersonal, dimension of sexuality.

The price to be paid in order to displace negative feelings of discomfort, disgust, and pain into a positive polarity, *as if* they were experienced as pleasant, is very high, being in fact *dissociation*. "I am not here. This isn't happening"[13] may be considered a concise and effective way to describe the attitude that is needed by women in order to stride in the direction of the *non-differentiated*.[14] Dissociation starts here as a more or less conscious effort to distance themselves from the hardship of what they experience with their senses during the porn shoot.

While the spectator/voyeur is comfortably sitting at home in front of his computer, and prepares to experience the *phantom* of the porn scene only through sight and hearing, porn performers are immersed in a complete sensorial experience; especially actresses, involved in the aforementioned effort of the displacement of negative sensations into a positive polarity, must tolerate possibly distasteful smells, unpleasant tastes, and various degrees of physical discomfort detected by the other senses, for dozens of minutes. Dissociation could represent the only way to stand what is going on for the time required.

This more or less conscious effort may progressively overlap with a more unconscious defence, aimed at keeping their deeper emotional responses at bay, afterwards. The haunting nature of a porn scene previously described,[15] that quality of certain images to obsess and harass the spectator, due to their unsettling and disturbing content, could reasonably affect porn actresses as well, who actually experience those very scenes in reality, with all their five senses.

The visual memories of the scene, its images, summed to all the bodily sensations connected to the experience itself, and most of all the "feeling-tone" associated with the whole situation they had to undergo, could configure what in Jungian terms we define as an "autonomous complex".

On one side, the whole experience has to be faced with a dissociative, conscious attitude, while on the other, the complex (that is, the set of different elements, unified by a "feeling-tone"), is dissociated as well, and possibly repressed. Hence, it is highly probable that the complex as such can be reactivated in a subsequent moment, triggered by other life situations, and the visual, sensorial, and emotional contents of the dissociated experience can come back, in the form of a haunting memory, or of an unsettling flashback.

Dealing with a powerful, numinous element like sexuality, moving on the *spectrum* towards the *non-differentiated*, immersed in the extreme no-limits style that informs our current era, women would need dissociation, in order to bear the physical and the emotional weight of what they perform, to a degree that is absolutely unknown to male performers.

The haunting quality of porn experiences can entail the need of dissociation and its own rooting as a structural element of the psyche of female performers. The price for entering the realm of the sacred and of the non-differentiated can definitely be extremely high for a woman: dissociation can be experienced as a loss of the soul, and may bring a feeling of disunity and fragmentation.

The frame of sacrality and divinity has vanished, we said.

The goddesses are inexorably lost.

The unconscious nostalgia for the sacred, though, has not subsided, and looks for new ways to quench its thirst of meaning, in many fields of our de-animated era.

To the ancient goddess of love and sex, astray in the mists of time, corresponds now an unaware desire for what our psyche needed through their presence.

Porn actresses may embody the medium to enter what used to be the realm of the sacred.

They sometimes succeed in representing such numinous content for a brief trice of grace and divinity, expressed mostly through their glance, their smile, and their facial expressions. But they pay a very painful price for gifting the spectator of this trice, even more painful because it is not acknowledged and valued: by male porn performers, by the spectators, by women in general, and by girls and women in porn themselves, either unaware of their power, or, at times, inflated by it in ways that make them blind to their own radiance.

Worshipping the goddesses, or their sacred representatives, definitely belongs to past eras. Nevertheless, its possible counterparts in the current desacralised epoch could be admiration, veneration (an ancient verb that still speaks to us of Venus Aphrodite), and a painful gratitude to the women who offer a glimpse of grace, in a world that almost always neglects it.[16]

The various shadows of Western culture, though, often suffocate this glimpse, in the very moment of its apparition. The shadow of technology that dominates our lives, for instance, encourages emotional dissociation and addiction; the shadow of consumerism emphasises an empty seduction, feeding a permanent dissatisfaction, and transforms each of us into mere cogs of a mechanism, whose goals we must ignore; the shadow of the human, too human destructiveness still emerges in manifold ways; the shadow of patriarchy, with its miserable power issues, seems far from transforming into higher levels of awareness; the shadow of our no-limits mentality, with its "logic of the cancer" colours every aspect of our Western world, threatening our existence. All these and more shadows often concur to kill the apparition of grace, numinosity, and sacrality, paradoxically present at the very core of porn too.

Porn imagery could be considered one of the post-modern stages where grace winks, and immediately disappears, under its consumerist degeneration, similarly to what happens in many forms of art as well.

Were we able to become deeply aware of all the shadows previously listed, to integrate them, and to gain momentum in order to go beyond them, so to say, even porn could become something else.

It could become a place where female performers can embody aspects traditionally belonging to the area of the sacred, and gift the world with glimpses of grace, being careful not to pay too high a price.

It could become a place where male performers give up the patriarchal antics, and open themselves up to look for the correspondent form of sacrality possible to masculinity.

It could become a place of inspiration for spectators, who would no more be mere consumers and voyeurs, devoid of any ethical responsibility for what they watch, but human beings who will try to embody porn in their own lives, as a real experience of the pristine joy of the body.

It could become a place that may teach human beings to approach the *non-differentiated* waiving the *as if* quality in its fake aspects of displacement, and preserving it in the acceptance of a genuine form of playing.

Porn could become a place where grace is not the swan-song of a dying woman's soul, but a divine quality, evoked, embodied, and accordingly worshipped by those who would be deeply tuned on it.

Such a place, in current porn, does exist, if briefly, in those rare encounters between a more aware need of the sacred, experienced in an adult way, and the mostly unaware gifts, painfully offered by the descendants of the lost goddesses.

NOTES

Front Matter

1. See the article *Femministe in lite sul fronte del porno*, published in *Corriere della Sera* (10 June 2012), p. 8.
2. Bondage, Dominance, Sadism, Masochism.
3. The first example could be considered John Cleland's erotic novel *Fanny Hill* (1748), originally entitled *Memoirs of a Woman of Pleasure*.

Chapter One

1. The 1896 French movie *Douche après le Bain* is the first known movie portraying sexual content. The Argentinian movie *El Sartorio*, dating back to 1907, showed a blow job, sixty-nine, and close-up images of penetration.
2. We can mention here the Wien-based company Saturn, which produced erotic movies, shown during so-called *Herrenabende* (evenings for gentlemen), in the first decade after 1900.
3. 1902–1992.
4. The chosen English title is "The Obsolescence of Man", although "The Obsolescence of Human Being" might have been more appropriate. It's obviously impossible to summarise here all the pivotal elements of Anders' reflections, albeit I will refer to some of them in the present work.

The English reader may check the links https://libcom.org/library/obsolescence-man-volume-2-günther-anders and https://libcom.org/library/obsolescence-man-volume-i-part-two-"-world-phantom-matrix-philosophical-considerations-r

Unfortunately, these web documents do not show page numbers. In the present work, Anders' quotations are taken from these links, but I refer to the pages and the year of publication of the Italian edition, listed in the references.

5. In reality, we are paying a very high price, on many levels, from economical to environmental.
6. In Anders' words, "no means is only a means".
7. See in this regard the essay entitled "Stepping up to a more general level" at the link https://libcom.org/library/chapter-5-stepping-more-general-level
8. "Drug addiction is the model for today's needs; which is to say that needs owe their 'existence' and their 'nature' to the physical existence of particular commodities" (Anders, ibid.).

Chapter Two

1. In this regard, see the whole essay "The world delivered to your home" at the link https://libcom.org/library/chapter-1-world-delivered-your-home.
2. The 1928 fantasy of Georges Bataille, when Simone inserts in her pussy one of the eyes of Don Aminado, the young priest she seduces and kills, while keeping on fucking with the unknown narrator of the story, finds here a symbolic realisation. See G. Bataille (1979), *Story of the Eye*, Marion Boyars. The dead eye that cannot see is now transformed into the camera eye that enables us to see.
3. *"Learn to need what is offered for sale!"*, Anders mocks. See the essay "The Matrix", at the link https://libcom.org/library/chapter-4-matrix
4. See Herman, S. E., & Chomsky, N. (1988). *Manufacturing Consent: The Political Economy of the Mass Media*. New York: Pantheon Books.

Chapter Four

1. According to the data of the Embassy of the Republic of Kenya in Japan, Kenya is the largest supplier of flowers to the European Union: 65 per cent of the flowers Kenya exports go to Holland, another 25 per cent to the UK. See http://www.kenyarep-jp.com/business/industry/f_market_e.html
2. 518.000 m^2, or 5,57 million square feet; source Wikipedia.

3. For six years, I did not own a car, using only a bicycle or public transportation in the Helsinki area. I have had no TV since 2007, and no TV-related devices from before then. Never in my life have I possessed any electronic device for entertainment. I buy flowers very rarely, and avoid buying a lot of other goods in general. I try to buy only seasonal fruit, where possible from countries that are close to Finland. I seldom buy meat, and never fish.

   Nevertheless, I feel the impact of my efforts is basically useless. I have to eat, I have to buy clothes and shoes, I enjoy having a drink or a dinner every now and then, I love musical instruments, I travel for lecturing and with my family when it's possible.

   The idea that more and more people may become aware and critical consumers, and help to reduce the waste of resources, the exploitation of the land, the sea, and the people, looks like trying to stop a tsunami with bare hands. Besides, the technological, productive, and capitalistic apparatus has often proven to be able to include in its consumerist model everything, green economy as well.

4. The explicit invitation of these websites is to subscribe and pay their fees, "in order to ensure the possibility to continue producing porn material of the best quality".

5. "Gang bang" is the name of a porn genre where one girl or woman is fucked by several men at the same time. In this particular scene, a girl in a doggy-style position was brutally penetrated by two cocks at the same time in her ass, while she was violently throat-fucked by a third cock. Essentially, three men were penetrating her, while a further four or five men, all very muscled, were around her in circle, waiting for their turn, while jerking off. None of the men's faces were visible; one could see only the woman, at the very centre of the scene (in this regard, see Chapter Nine).

   The girl was barely able to manage and control the pain from the harsh penetrations, both in her ass and in her throat, when a man put his hand to her throat. For several seconds, she could not breathe, while brutally penetrated. The man stopped smothering her, only to shout at her sarcastically "Hey, are you still with us?", follow by the crass laughter of the other beheaded men. The girl appeared confused, numb: she was not acting, rather was really stunned and disoriented. Coming across such a scene, and its boorish macho dominating attitude, evoked in me the deepest rage.

Chapter Five

1. In this regard, see Zoja, L., *Growth and Guilt: Psychology and the Limits of Development*. London: Routledge, and also the eighth chapter of my

book *The Labyrinth of Possibility*, entitled *Closing Chords—Possibility and Limit* (pp. 85–97).
2. For a deeper view on this epochal rapture and some of its possible consequences, see my paper *The Quest for Meaning after the End of Meaning*, in the Appendix.
3. It is never too obvious to notice that an original thread ties up death and sexuality. If death did not exist, sexuality would not have been necessary. Sexuality can always be considered an answer to the existence of death, even when its procreative aim is not in the foreground. Sexuality is a hymn to life and to its continuance, in a large part of porn as well, albeit often unconsciously.
4. See in this regard Zoja, L. (2001). *The Father: Historical, Psychological, and Cultural Perspectives*. Hove: Brunner-Routledge.
5. See in this regard Giegerich, W. (2004). *The End of Meaning and the Birth of Man*. London: The Guild of Pastoral Psychology.
6. Directed by Gérard Damiano, Arrow production, 1972.
7. Linda Lovelace performs these extreme blowjobs herself, deciding how and when to swallow down the penises of the actors. We are far from the brutal throat-fucking of current porn, where the actress has to bear for several tens of minutes violent insertions of the cock down her throat, passively taken, kept breathless for seconds, even, her face covered with her own deep saliva, and sometimes her own retching, until men eventually come in her mouth and on her face, to her great relief.
8. The most common sex scene sequence, between an actor and an actress, starts with a blowjob (or a more brutal throat-fuck), continues with vaginal penetration, and most of all anal sex, often very raw and aimed at anal gaping; then it continues showing the alternation of anal sex and blowjob (the so-called "ass to mouth"), and eventually the actor's coming in the woman's open mouth and/or on her face ("facial", "cumshot"). I would maintain that this is the most common pattern in current internet porn, with some slight variations. Elements aimed at the woman's pleasure, like petting, caressing, licking tits and nipples, cunnilingus, anal rimming, are often notably missing, unless the scene is a threesome (one man and two women/girls), and all these elements are performed between the women.
9. For a good example of extreme performances for their own sake, see Annette Schwartz, a German porn actress who acted in almost three hundred porn films since the age of eighteen, and who brands herself as "The cum piss slut" (http://totallyannette.tumblr.com), or any trailer in the website www.legalporn.com
10. The use of any kind of body fluid (saliva, sperm, urine, female squirt, vomit even) as sexual material to be received abundantly in the woman's mouth, and enjoyed, shared, or swallowed, the insertion of dildos

and objects of any dimension in every orifice, painful double and triple penetrations, unbelievable vaginal and anal dilatations, lesbian sex games with anal prolapses, violent throat-fucking and choking blowjobs, inundating bukkakes, are only some examples.

Chapter Six

1. By *feminine* I intend here the sensitivity to emotions and to the inner world, empathy, containment, sensuality, instinct, nature, earth, without forgetting that these features have been traditionally regarded as feminine within a patriarchal frame.
2. See in this regard the chapter entitled *The Patriarchal Sexual Legacy*, in TePaske (2008).
3. See Chapter Two of the present work.
4. See, for example, the accurate study conducted by Väestoliitto, The Family Federation of Finland, by Osmo Kontula, 2009.
5. There seems to be more awareness about men's use of porn among women of younger generations. Still, I remember the bride of a friend of mine, who stated that her husband would no longer need to watch porn movies, since he now had her. This statement showed her lack of awareness about the deeper reasons for watching porn, often totally independent from having or not a satisfying sexual relationship with a stable partner.
6. In this regard, I totally agree with TePaske's statement that "Any authentic change in a man's relationship with the anima or with women presupposes a deep confrontation with the masculine shadow" (2008, p. 27). A few lines further, he adds that "when a woman experiences the darker aspects of male sexuality, the relationship is over". I would rather suggest that to explore the shadow sides of male sexuality would be extremely important for a woman as well. Instead of denying the ascertained male's interest for porn, and feeling betrayed when she finds it out, a woman could actually know much more about her partner, as the porn he watches may reveal a lot about his shadow aspects. Getting to know them more deeply could be much better than to ignore them, for the sake of the relationship as well.
7. In the words of a married patient of mine, often dealing with anxiety attacks: "Of course, I would like to have flirts and sexual experiences with many women, but the way I am, it would create more tension than pleasure. Watching porn is an acceptable compromise between my desire for different experiences, and my intolerable anxiety about being possibly discovered by my wife, and about the expectations of a woman I may flirt with".

8. I invite the interested reader to check TePaske (2008), and also Zoja (2001).
9. In the majority of languages, the verbal forms referring to sexuality and desire show the ego as subjected to external forces that "take it", "kidnap it", "enchant it", "put a spell on it", "chain it", "overwhelm it", and so on. Together with myths, the language reveals our unconscious awareness that sex, passion, love are powerful elements, affecting our ego from the ouside.
10. Especially evident in the early years of porn, and every now and then in current porn productions, even.
11. As expressed by Winnicott in a famous passage: "The subject says to the object: "I have destroyed you", and the object is there to receive the communication. From now on the subject says, "Hullo, object! I've destroyed you." "I love you." "You have value for me because of your survival of my destruction of you." "While I am loving you, I am all the time destroying you in (unconscious) fantasy" (Winnicott, The use of an object and relating through identifications, *International Journal of Psychoanalysis*, 50, 1969).
12. In Chapter Nine, we will see how to diminish and despise women in porn, calling them "whore", "bitch", "slut", is not only the typical, mean patriarchal hypocrisy of despising what is actually valuable, desired and needed by every man, but may show the deepest envy for the power and the divinity of the feminine (a phenomenon much more evident than any penis envy, by the way). For a wider perspective on the feminine seen as evil and scapegoat of a sick patriarchal mentality, see also Neumann (1994).
13. The idol of my patient, in fact, was the Italian porn actor Rocco Siffredi, known for his annihilating approach to his female partners, as Piero Adamo (2004) defines it. In a typical scene of his, the girls are roughly and inexorably compelled to let him use and abuse every orifice of theirs for his sole pleasure. Nothing else matters. Another performer often appreciated by men like this patient of mine is Max Hardcore, famous for his clinical, cold sequence of actions that carefully exclude anything that could be pleasant for a woman. He never touches the actress' tits, never caresses her body, or licks her genitals, and very seldom penetrates her vagina. The typical pattern of his scenes consists of very brutal deep throat-fucking, alternated with pissing in the girl's mouth, often forcing her to swallow his pee, and of rough anal sex, methodically alternated with blowjobs, until he eventually comes in the girl's mouth, and pees again. The whole scene is performed by him just like a job, with a cold detachment, no particular signs of pleasure, and an obsessive repetition.

14. See Neumann, E. (1990). *Depth Psychology and a New Ethic.* Boston and London: Shambhala.
15. Many men have shared with me these kinds of experiences, of seeing for the first time as children the porn image of an opened, spread pussy. I also remember the astonishment of an adult patient of mine, telling how he came across a porn scene where a black woman was giving head to a horse, until the horse came with such a huge amount of sperm in her mouth that she was literally flooded by it. The scene actually disgusted him. He was also empathising with the girl, who must have performed the scene painfully surmounting her own disgust as well. Still, this scene haunted him, and he had to see it again. Until, to his own great dismay, the scene excited him, and he even masturbated himself watching it. The disgust for the scene eventually turned into feeling shame for his own excitement. Incidentally, sex scenes of women with animals (usually dogs, horses, and snakes) were quite common from the very beginning of mass porn, in the late 1960s and the 1970s, and continued as a niche genre until they were forbidden during the early 2000s. It must be noted that the initiative to forbid these kinds of scenes came from animal protection organisations, and were intended to prevent animal exploitation.

Chapter Seven

1. A remarkable exception is the very interesting book by Anderson (2002).
2. Interestingly enough, if we give credit to interviews and biographies of famous porn actors, the *as if* nature of women's performances is often neglected by them as well, and they apparently believe that actresses like what they experience. Despite the fact that they were there, on the scene, in factual touch with the girls and the women performers, they were not really *there*. Apparently, they were disconnected from the experience.
3. Jung (1931), pp. 45–46.
4. See in this regard Winnicott (1971).
5. Kontula mentions that in studies on childhood sexual games, these are categorised as 1) playing house, 2) touching, 3) playing doctor, 4) playing at being animals, 5) actual sex play, closely resembling adult sexual experiences. See Kontula (2009).

Chapter Eight

1. See Kontula (2009).
2. In this regard, I would quote Kontula, where he maintains that "Something that is not in one's own interest is easy to reject and disapprove"

(2009, p. 65); Moore as well underlines that "It doesn't do us much good to maintain public disapproval of sexual imagery while private appeal to it is so widespread and compulsive" (1999, p. 87).

3. Excluding the niche of the "gynaecological" genre, with its focus on internal close-ups and abundant use of specula and medical retractors, this judgement overlooks the fact that videos showing too long-lasting close-ups of the genitals only are usually rated negatively by the users themselves, and considered bad porn.

4. It's not uncommon that porn videos appear repetitive, using the same images and showing the same structure. But it shouldn't be forgotten that the spectator watches those images out of sexual desire: with the same logic, eating could also be deemed as a repetitive activity, as it consists of the very same gestures, every meal. But a hungry person would absolutely enjoy this repetitive action.

5. Regazzoni (2010) underlines that *degradation* has the meaning of losing rank/grade/level, and maintains that porn shows a metamorphosis of the subjects, a process towards the "grade zero" of subjectivity. This process of de-gradation of the subjects would correspond to Jacques Derrida's concept of *deconstruction*. In porn, we would witness the deconstruction of subjectivity. I reckon that this concept actually applies on a deeper level only to women in porn.

6. Unless one is married to the idea of men as evil, violent, and brutal by nature, as some anti-porn feminists vehemently have claimed.

7. Jenna Jameson, one of the most famous American professional porn stars, warmly advises every girl or woman who is going to shoot a porn scene never to go alone to the set. The presence of someone else seems to her fundamental, while negotiating the contract details before the scene (what she is willing to do, what she does not want to do, how much to be paid for each action, etc.), and in order to have support during and, most of all, after the scene-shooting. The risk of not taking this precaution is to live through a deeply humiliating experience, where perfect strangers use her, maybe hurt her, and defile her, calling her "slut", "bitch", "whore", for endless minutes that seem hours. The fictional nature of the porn scene is easily overshadowed, because actually what is going on is absolutely real, for the performers. See Jameson & Strauss (2006).

8. For instance, tryteens.com, teachmyass.com, doubletamedteens.com, gag-n-gape.com

9. In a genre generally called "old and young", for example, the female performer, often a very young girl, tries to abolish the differences, and seems to hanker to suck the flabby cocks of men in their seventies or older, craving to be besmirched in her face by a luscious load

of sperm (and, right after, of piss), instead of being repelled by it. The uglier and sleasier the old men are, the more the girl can try to head towards the *non-differentiated*, in a sort of "Beauty and the Beast" frame. In another genre, often dubbed "moms and teens", there is the corresponding performance in a lesbo version, between young, beautiful girls and unattractive older ladies. In both genres, what should be disgusting is performed *as if* it were wondrous.

In many videos, though, the girls partially fail, and disgust and loathing visibly crop up, to the pleasure of the more sadistic-oriented shadow elements in some men's psychic landscapes.

10. Penetrations are alternated between mouth, vagina, and anus of the actresses, in their total equivalence, and every fluid, from saliva to sperm, from female ejaculations to piss (in extreme cases, even vomit) are all received by the actresses in all their orifices, *as if* it were divine ambrosia, to be enjoyed, shared, spread, drunk.
11. On the side of disgust, for instance, mainstream porn normally requires girls and women to perform lesbo scenes (pussy licking, ass licking, rimming, squirting, piss drinking, ass to mouth with dildos, anal gaping, fisting, and so on) when they are neither lesbians nor bisexual, or even with women of any age and physical appearance. Threesome scenes normally require some degree of lesbian sex as well, together with progressively more demanding scenes, like ass to mouth blow jobs, anal gape licking, cum drinking from the other woman's ass, cum sharing, and so on. Gang bangs and *bukkake* are genres where women have to drink and swallow an enormous load of sperm from several men, coming one after the other, the sperm poured either directly in their mouths, or into a glass, to be emptied afterwards.

   On the side of pain, besides the previously mentioned throat-fucking, stands the nowadays common practice of dry anal penetration, which allows a quicker and wider dilatation (anal gape) to be shown, but that is reportedly very painful for the actresses. In threesome scenes between a girl or a woman and two or more men, double penetration is quite common in current mainstream porn. The French porn actress Rafaela Anderson (2002) describes it as so painful that she fainted the first time she had to perform it. Close-ups of the genitals are used, in such cases, in order to avoid showing the unmistakable pain expressions of the female performer, or her tears and uncontrollable crying. However, due to the similarity between facial expressions of pain and of pleasure, the scenes often keep showing the woman's face. It would not take an exceptional sensitivity to understand from the girls' expressions and moaning whether

pain exceeds the level they can actually bear. Male actors, however, apparently ignore (sometimes on purpose) these clear signs of pain, and the actresses' signals to ease their discomfort. In such cases, the *as if* quality and the fictional displacement cannot take place, and the scene takes the form of an openly brutal performance.
12. See the end of Chapter Five.
13. As stated by Heraclitus, in fragment 102, "To a god all things are fair and good and right, but men hold some things wrong and some right".
14. See, in this regard, the aforementioned book by Te Paske, *Sexuality and the Religious Imagination*, and *The Soul of Sex*, by Thomas Moore.
15. In the Old Testament, for instance, *The Song of Songs* makes extensive use of sensual, erotic imagery, while describing the manifold relationship between human beings and God.
16. Yow, B. (1996). *Pink Madness*, by James Hillman, *Psychological Perspectives: A Quarterly Journal of Jungian Thought*, 33(1): 157.
17. Ibid., p. 155.
18. Ibid., pp. 156–157.
19. Once again, this portrait of porn is at odds with the deep fascination that so many people admit to having, as far as it is possible to declare it anonymously.
20. "Eroticism can be raised to its highest for in service of the divine, as in the erotic poetry of Rumi, the ecstatic reveries of the Sufis, or the sensuality of the *Kama Sutra*" (Yow, 1996, p. 155), as well in erotic paintings and photography.
21. Hesiod, Theogony, 176ff (translation Evelyn-White).
22. See, in this regard, Kerényi, K. (1999). *Goddesses of Sun and Moon*, Washington: Spring Publications.

Chapter Nine

1. A comparison by analogy of some of the most difficult scenes, performed by girls and women in porn, could be a man receiving in his mouth a good load of menstrual blood, oozing from the pussy of one or more actresses, rinsing his mouth with it, sharing it with another man while kissing him wildly, and eventually swallowing it all, both men showing excitement and enthusiasm.
2. Or at least very different. We should wonder what the masculine counterpart to the women's entering the realm of the sacred, while moving towards *non-differentiation*, could be.
3. See, in this regard, any of the scenes performed by Marina Ann Hantzis, aka Sasha Gray. Debuting at the age of eighteen, she is credited for two hundred and seventy-one films shot in five years of her career as a porn

actress, after which she decided to leave the adult movies environment, in favour of writing books and working in the mainstream movie and in the music industries. Her performances are close to the more elevated degrees of the *spectrum* towards the *non-differentiated*. Nevertheless, she is apparently masterfully managing the *displacement* of feelings, and never gives the impression of succumbing to, or being diminished by, the poor behaviour of the male performers she acts with. Her standing in the central position of the stage, radiant and shining, while performing very extreme actions *as if* they were wondrous, makes her a prototype of the successful porn actress, also in the sense we are exploring here. She also seems to be pretty aware of her potency and numinosity.

4. See, for example, Jameson & Strauss (2004), Ovidie (2002), Despentes (2007), and most of all Anderson (2001). After dozens of minutes of brutal and demeaning actions, the actresses' joyousness for facial ejaculations is genuine and pristine, not because they would enjoy tasting sperm as if it were nectar of the gods, but because men's cumshots often signal the awaited end of a torment.
5. A fucking machine consists of a mechanical plunger, or piston, connected to an electric engine, ending with a dildo or a realistic rubber cock. The actress lets the dildo penetrate her pussy or ass, at different speeds, and for the time wanted, for the joy of transhumanism fans.
6. See Qualls-Corbett (1988).
7. In this regard, see the essay in the Appendix.
8. See Zoja (2000).
9. See, in this regard, my article entitled "The Individuation Process in Post-Modernity", *Psychological Perspectives*, 59(4): 461–472 (2016).
10. In this regard, I refer the reader once more to the Appendix at the end of this book.
11. A good example could be a scene performed by the aforementioned Annette Schwartz, where she inserted a plastic funnel in her ass, and three different men were pissing into it. After keeping this big load of urine inside her for a while, she poured it from her ass, directly into a big glass jug, only to start drinking it, and swallowing. After some gulps, she clearly had to control her retching. An actor commented that maybe she could avoid doing it, but she testily replied: "No! I have to!", as if she were challenging herself. Other germane examples of a similar kind of *hybris* are anal fisting, and the anal insertion of monster dildos or objects that are huge beyond all reason.
12. I have witnessed myself this genuine male gratitude, on the occasion of an exhibition by Paola Suhonen, hosted at Helsinki Taidehalli (Art Hall of Helsinki), on 3 December 2016. The exhibition, entitled *Love on the Road*, was focused on the American porn actress Nina Hartley, and displayed pictures and videos of her, plus other material inspired by her. At the opening

of the exhibition, Nina Hartley herself was present, and anyone could sit on a couch with her, and kiss her, while being filmed and photographed by Paola Suhonen, for the sake of an installation to be added to the exhibition. Quite surprisingly, many women of all ages were queueing to kiss the famous porn star; many of them were as kindled by the power of Nina's sexual energy, and for a few moments became more feminine, sexy, and hot than they appeared to be while queueing. Among men, I saw more than one who hugged Nina with affection, their eyes lost in her charming green eyes, wearing the facial expression of the child who meets the fairy of their dreams. A sincere gratitude for what Nina had given them through years of porn movies was painted on their joyful, touched faces. And on her side, Nina had the most affectionate attention to all of them, with an attitude that felt genuine, very sweet, and at time maternal.
13. "That there, that's not me", "In a little while, I'll be gone. The moment already passed. Yeah it's gone. And I am not here. This isn't happening" are some lyrics from the song *How to Disappear Completely*, by Radiohead. I aver these words may be a careful description of the type of dissociation possibly needed by girls and women in porn.
14. We underline once again that nothing like this is requested of male performers in porn.
15. See Chapter Six.
16. The gratitude would be painful because it would acknowledge the discomfort experienced by girls and women in order to convey and embody that glimpse of grace, so needed in our dry times.

REFERENCES

Adamo, P. (2004). *Il porno di massa. Percorsi dell'hard contemporaneo*. Milano: Raffaello Cortina Editore.

Anders, G. (2007a). *L'uomo è antiquato, Vol. 1: Considerazioni sull'anima nell'epoca della seconda rivoluzione industriale*. Torino: Universale Bollati Boringhieri. [Original edition: Anders, G. (1956). *Die Antiquiertheit des Menschen, Band I: Über die Seele im Zeitalter der zweiten industriellen Revolution*. München: Verlag C. H. Bech.]

Anders, G. (2007b). *L'uomo è antiquato, Vol. 2: Sulla distruzione della vita nell'epoca della terza rivoluzione industriale*. Torino: Universale Bollati Boringhieri. [Original edition: Anders, G. (1980). *Die Antiquiertheit des Menschen, Band II: Über die Zerstörung des Lebens im Zeitalter der dritten industriellen Revolution*. München: Verlag C. H. Bech.]

Anderson, R. (2002). *Hard*. Parma: Guanda. [Original edition: Anderson, R. (2001). *Hard*. Paris: Grasset & Fasquelle.]

Arendt, H. (1963). *Eichmann in Jerusalem: A Report on the Banality of Evil*. New York: Viking Press.

Bauman, Z. (2003). *Liquid Love: On the Frailty of Human Bonds*. Cambridge: Polity Press.

Bauman, Z. (2007). *Liquid Times: Living in an Age of Uncertainty*. Cambridge: Polity Press.

Bonazzi, M., & Cappa, F. (a cura di) (2010). *Pop Porn. Critica dell'immaginario porno*. Milano: et al. Edizioni.
Ciuffoli, E. (2006). *XXX. Corpo, porno, web*. Milano: Costa & Nolan.
Despentes, V. (2007). *King Kong Girl*. Torino: Einaudi. [Original edition: Despentes, V. (2006). *King Kong théorie*. Paris: Grasset & Fasquelle.]
Eliade, M. (2006). *Il sacro e il profano*. Torino: Bollati Boringhieri. [Original edition: Eliade, M. (1965). *Le sacré et le profane*. Paris: Gallinard.]
Eliade, M. (2015). *Sull'erotica mistica indiana e altri scritti*. Torino: Bollati Boringhieri. [Original edition: Eliade, M. (1987). *Sur l'érotique mystique indienne*. Paris: Éditions de l'Herne.]
Fini, M. (2000). *Di[zion]ario erotico*. Venezia: Marsilio.
Ford, L. (2010). *Storia di XXX. 100 anni di sesso nei film*. Bologna: Odoya. [Original edition: Ford, L. (1999). *A History of X. 100 Years of Sex in Films*. New York: Prometheus Books.]
Giegerich, W. (2004). *The End of Meaning and the Birth of Man*. London: The Guild of Pastoral Psychology.
Girard, R. (1986). *The Scapegoat*. Baltimore: The John Hopkins University Press.
Jameson, J., & Strauss, N. (2006). *Vita da pornostar*. Milano: RCS. [Original edition: Jameson, J., & Strauss, N. (2004). *How To Make Love Like a Pornstar*. New York: HarperCollins.]
Jung, C. G. (1991). *Aion*. In: *Collected Works*, Vol. 9. London: Routledge & Kegan Paul.
Kontula, O. (2009). *Between Sexual Desire and Reality: The Evolution of Sex in Finland*. Publication of The Population Research Institute D 49/2009. Helsinki: Vammalan Kirjapaino OY.
Moore, T. (1999). *The Soul of Sex: Cultivating Life as an Act of Love*. New York: HarperPerennial.
Neumann, E. (1994). *The Fear of the Feminine and Other Essays on Feminine Psychology*. Bollingen Series LXI 4. Princeton: Princeton University Press.
Ovidie (2003). *Porno Manifesto. Storia di una passione proibita*. Milano: Baldini & Castoldi. [Original edition: Ovidie (2002). *Porno Manifesto*. Paris: Flammarion.]
Paul, P. (2007). *Pornopotere. Come l'industria porno sta trasformando la nostra vita*. Milano: orme editori. [Original edition: Paul, P. (2005). *Pornified: How Pornography Is Damaging Our Lives, Our Relationships and Our Families*. New York: Times Books.]
Qualls-Corbett, N. (1988). *The Sacred Prostitute. Eternal Aspect of the Feminine*. Toronto: Inner City Books.
Regazzoni, S. (2010). *Pornosofia. Filosofia del pop porno*. Milano: Salani.
TePaske, B. (2008). *Sexuality and the Religious Imagination*. New Orleans: Spring Journal.

Tricarico, G. (2014). *The Labyrinth of Possibility: A Therapeutic Factor in Analytical Practice*. London: Karnac Books.

Tricarico, G. (2016). *The Individuation Process in Post-Modernity, Psychological Perspectives: A Quarterly Journal of Jungian Thought*, 59(4): 461–472.

Winnicott, D. W. (1971). *Playing and Reality*. London: Routledge.

Yow, B. (1996). *Pink Madness*, by James Hillman. *Psychological Perspectives: A Quarterly Journal of Jungian Thought, 33(1)*: 154–157.

Zoja, L. (1995). *Growth and Guilt: Psychology and the Limits of Development*. London: Routledge.

Zoja, L. (2000). *Drugs, Addiction, and Initiation: The Modern Search for Ritual*. Einsiedeln: Daimon Verlag.

Zoja, L. (2001). *The Father: Historical, Psychological, and Cultural Perspectives*. Hove: Brunner-Routledge.

APPENDIX

The quest for meaning after the end of meaning*

An epochal rupture

The reflections explored in these pages start from acknowledging a passage in the history of Western consciousness. This passage, or better, rupture, becomes more visible in the second half of the nineteenth century, over a period of about a hundred and fifty years, during which the Enlightenment, the Industrial Revolution, and a vertiginous acceleration of technological development came to represent the warp and weft of the modern era.

Prior to modernity, myths, religions, and metaphysics had undoubtedly expressed the logic of the absolute containment in life. For millennia, human life had experienced the conscious awareness of being wrapped up in some form of containment: in Nature; in *Midgard* (our

---

*This paper was presented at the Second Conference of the ISPDI (The International Society for Psychology as the Discipline of Interiority), hosted in Berlin, between 19 and 21 July 2014.

I have included this paper in the present work, although it does not deal with porn, in order to illustrate some of the coordinates of the current era, that is the background of porn as a mass phenomenon.

land, a place between the underworld and heaven, the earth and the sky); in the ancient customs and traditions of the mythical ancestors; in the horizon of Fate; in the gods', and eventually, in God's will.

As Wolfgang Giegerich aptly puts it, a sense of metaphysical "in-ness" has always contained human existence absolutely:[1] in the pre-modern ages, human beings were not born directly into their environment, but into "myths, meanings, ideas, images, words, creeds, theories, traditions".[2] From the moment they were born, individuals were immediately enveloped by these different frames of meaning.

This realisation allows Giegerich to state that man, despite to his literal biological birth, was basically unborn, because he had logically never left this in-ness in a metaphysical womb of meaning. Contained in a virtual uterus, invisible as such, in the spiritual womb of the mind, of the soul, of the concepts and the language, man could be still "upward looking to the gods, his world parents or to God, his Father",[3] and remain in a sort of "metaphysical childhood".

But during the modern age, the history of consciousness sees an epochal rupture: modernity sees human beings emerging from their containment in a womb, from the ocean of meaning given *a priori*. Accordingly, the individuals lose their myths and their symbols, leave their father and mother behind, hatch from the "egg" of in-ness, so to say, and for the first time ever, find themselves out in the open, in a condition of metaphysical nakedness.

Post-modernity starts when humankind realises itself to be undeniably *extra ecclesiam et naturam*, abandoned to what Jung called the "illimitable loneliness of man".[4]

This rupture, which Giegerich describes as the real birth of man, appears to be the outcome of a long process, the upshot of the internal logic of the history of the Western world, in Martin Heidegger's words.[5]

The starting point of this process would date back to the Greek meaning of "becoming", according to the philosopher Emanuele Severino.[6] He suggests that the poet and philosopher Giacomo Leopardi (1798–1837) was the first thinker in Western culture who detected the nihilistic essence of modernity, some decades before Friedrich Nietzsche. The latter clearly caught the epochal rupture while it was happening, stating that God was dead, and that all the supreme values had lost every value.

The essence of the philosophical thought of the eighteenth and nineteenth centuries, together with the increasing power of the scientific-technological apparatus, has brought the omnipotent domination of technology over every aspect of human life.

In fact, the main feature of the Western world, since Enlightenment and the Industrial Revolution, consists of a progressive repression of limits and in its consequent omnipotent mentality.[7]

No absolute Truth, no immutabile principles, in other words no metaphysical limit, are the pre-conditions for technology to reach a status of omnipotence.

The need of no limits requires that every *epistéme* (literally what stands on its own feet, without any external support) necessarily fades away, leaving room to a multiplicity of relative truths and to a polytheism of values.

When every limit is denied and repressed, we see the overcoming of any form of containment, because limit, from Latin *limes*, means exactly border, boundary. In this regard, it's more understandable "why the last two centuries had to experience a loss of meaning, a sense of alienation and nihilism",[8] because the meaning of "meaning" was given by the containment itself, by the embeddedness, by the in-ness.

Filling up the void sky after God's death, technology, however, does not offer any particular frame of meaning, its goals being just to expand infinitely the potential to reach goals and to function.[9]

During the early decades of the twentieth century, several authors and thinkers, including C. G. Jung, acknowledged the lack of meaning of modern life would correspond to the perception of the epochal rupture described here. Max Weber dubbed the contemporary world as "disenchanted", implying a previous enchantment that has come to some sort of an end; Wolfgang Pauli referred to the "de-animation" of the physical world, pointing out that the *anima*, the soul, has disappeared, leaving our modern word de-animated, that is, without *anima*; Mircea Eliade spoke of "desacralisation", to underline that the sacred eclipsed in favour of a profane attitude, and Jung also stated that "There are no longer gods whom we could invoke to help us".[10]

As a consequence to this disenchantment and this de-animation of the world, apparently Jung's aim became to restore meaning, and to retrieve what he called "symbolic life".

In Giegerich's opinion, though, the collective unconscious and its archetypal contents, *in primis* the Self, as a renewed version of God, might be seen as a recreation of a new form of containment, an attempt to deny the birth of man and to restore something that had been lost.[11]

From the point of view of the history of consciousness, Giegerich considers the epochal rupture of the end of any containment and its consequent metaphysical nakedness the very beginning of a new logic form of being-in-the world, that of "metaphysical adulthood", a form that should be embraced wholeheartedly.

I leave to the reader the task of exploring in a deeper way the contrast between Jung and Giegerich on this specific point.

At this point, let's be content with the terms of the problem: the death of God, the central position of technology and science in the post-modern world, the fading of every absolute truth and its consequent relativism appear to be the coordinates of the spirit of our time.

Acknowledging the *zeitgeist* of post-modernity compels us to face its logic consequences, and stand up to large-scale theoretical and clinical difficulties. How can we reconcile the end of in-ness with the acute need for frames of meaning for the suffering of our patients, and of human beings in general?

As analysts, if we make our own frames of meaning explicit, would they still stand in the light of the epochal rupture previously portrayed? Although as clinicians, exploring the psyche, we have the strongest impression to deal with something *other* from consciousness, something autonomous, pursuing goals, can we continue in our clinical practice naively, and acritically trust in a sort of secular substitute of God, which apparently is the Jungian Self, and in its prospective and teleological aims?

These and further questions might sound philosophical, at first view, but as far as I can see, they hold a sharp and deep clinical relevance.

Meeting the Evil in the post-modern era: a Job Experience *and* The Place

Seizing the problem from a more clinical point of view, let's mention the case of Amanda Wilhelmina. At the age of forty-three, her four-month-old daughter Wappu Kyllikki dies. Eleven days later, her husband dies as well, leaving Amanda with her only daughter Aino Charlotta, who at that time was four years old. Aino Charlotta herself dies at the age of thirteen, when Amanda is only fifty-two. Amanda Wilhelmina will die thirty-four years later, eighty-six years old, in 1939.

I found Amanda's family tomb by chance, during one of my walks through the beautiful cemetery of Hietaniemi, which lies in silence, lapped by the sea, in the centre of Helsinki. The tombstone of the family reports in cold dates the wounds of lives swallowed by time, more than a hundred years ago. My first thought, in front of Amanda's tomb, was: what if she were a patient of mine, now, in the beginning of the third millennium?

Hopefully, in the time when she lived, when those terrible losses occurred, she could still count on some frame of meaning. A religious frame probably helped her to situate those losses into a bigger picture. And surely, the death of children and of adults, due to epidemic diseases, was a much more common event at the end of the nineteenth century.

But how could a modern patient, a woman I might meet today in my practice room, living in the age of omnipotence and of the end of containment, cope with the same kinds of experiences? She would be at least desperate, if not angry. Intensely depressed, if not suicidal. As therapists, we might try to help her *do* something to go on, beyond the losses, finding some answer to the question "how?": how to survive the pain, how to cope with her life, how to put her soul's pieces together, how to carry on.

But what if she raised the question "why?". This very question has always been highly problematic, even when the individual was still embedded in the in-ness: confronting the unintelligible evil, the puzzling suffering of the righteous, the unthinkable pain, has always creaked the structure of in-ness, and heavily shaken its foundations.

I find it hard to believe that, until the nineteenth century, the issue of meaning of life, when the individual was to encounter the radical Evil, was not in the foreground, as if it was just self-evident. As we know, the first clear example of this encounter, in the Western tradition, is the Book of Job.

Two thousand years of theodicy, and countless thinkers, authors, and philosophers touched by the question, testify to the wound inflicted in the shell of in-ness by the problem of Evil.

From the furious questions of Job, who was asking God to account for his intolerable misery, apparently coming from Him himself, to the disdainful words about the suffering of innocent children pronounced by Ivan in Dostoevski's *The Brothers Karamazov*,[12] we find numberless examples (Jung's "Answer to Job" being one of them) of the dramatic need of a frame of meaning when it comes to confronting the radical Evil.

Let's now imagine how meeting the Evil takes shape in the current era, the era of the repression of limits, and what consequences this meeting might have.

First of all, we define as a *Job Experience* the experience of an amount of pain exceeding a "good-enough" quantity. We can safely state that suffering is necessary to development and individuation, especially when pain concerns others, and when it is reasonably bearable; but when pain exceeds a "good-enough" quantity, we literally enter another territory, where pain is only felt as senseless and meaningless.

Unlike in past eras, a *Job Experience* nowadays can be simply facing an unexpected premature death, a heavily disabling illness, the loss of someone important, the insight of our extreme vulnerability, some acute or ongoing traumatic experiences.

Due to the massive repression of limits in every field (economics, science, technology, medicine, etc.), when a limit appears, it often takes the shape of a devastating experience, perceived as absolutely unfair, incomprehensible, and unbearable. The absence of any mythical, religious, or metaphysical frame of meaning makes a *Job Experience* in the post-modern era particularly inane and absurd. In the current era, death, as the main limit we all have to face, is only obscene, that is, *ob-scaena*, "out of the scene". When death and every other severe limit appear on the *scaena*, they are regarded as a scandal.

If the psyche does not succumb, the first consequence of a *Job Experience* is finding oneself in a different place from reality, a place other than the familiar *Midgard* we inhabit. This place being quite difficult to define precisely, we call it only *The Place*. In *The Place*, one can perceive time and perspective narrowing, sometimes in a claustrophobic way, while the prevailing emotion, besides pain and desperation, of course, is an intense, glossy rage.

Value judgements, while immersed in *The Place*, may take on the colour of a disenchanted disdain, similar to the tone we find in Giacomo Leopardi's *La Ginestra* (The Broom).

In the Book of Job, rage is the main feature of Job himself. It is his rage that compels God to account for His actions. When God appears, at the end of the book, He essentially emphasises the complete incapability of man of comprehending his designs. Obviously, Job could only surrender to the power of the Almighty, because he was still immersed in the in-ness.

But a "post-modern Job", in the same situation, would find the whole experience completely senseless, and would probably stare into God's eyes, eliciting much more than a paternal telling-off.

Ivan Karamazov's speech, previously mentioned, is certainly full of disdain and rage as well, but Dostoevski was still embedded in the in-ness of meaning, in his own personal existence, and God had to be ultimately seen as a good Father. It would have been extremely difficult to consider God both good and bad, in the best of cases.

Child analysts know very well children's need to preserve at all costs a good image of their parents, were they even sadists or abusers, to avoid a terrifying fragmentation of the whole psychic world. Embedded in the in-ness, the individual is basically like a child, who *must* keep a positive image of God, and cannot accept, despite all evidence, that Evil can only come from Him.

A post-modern Job, instead, immersed in *The Place*, could come to see quite clearly the co-existence of Good and Evil within God, and, most of all, God's ultimate responsibility for Evil.

While Giegerich believes that a *Job Experience* is not possible in the current era, because it would belong to a different form of being-in-the-world, to a time when man believed in a God above, and expected justice and a fair treatment,[13] I suggest that it is actually still possible.

The end of in-ness is definitely a collective passage of the Western soul, but on the individual level it probably takes the direct experience of a not-good-enough amount of pain in order to consciously start emerging from the previous forms of containment.

If being embedded in the in-ness corresponds to a stage of metaphysical childhood, as Giegerich avers, I suggest an individual might have to experience an intermediate stage, before accessing adulthood. I dub this intermediate stage *metaphysical teenage*.

Typical of this stage would be, among other things, a profound rage, and a radical hatred towards God or any *primum movens*.[14]

The hatred towards God could be at the same time hatred for the creation itself, because one can clearly see that the creation itself *is* the fall, as Simone Weil perfectly stated.

On one hand, man hates God, His *hybris*, His craving and lust in starting the creation, and shaping a universe essentially dominated by Evil/destruction. On the other hand, man can come to hate himself, the creature as well, in its resemblance to that inflated God, a creature able to do (quite rarely) good, but mostly to do evil. Disclosing the dominance of Evil in the creation and in the creator, begets a profound contempt and scorn.

The Ego, the mysterious and miraculous result of millions of years of evolution, is grounded on primary narcissism, psychoanalysis has taught us. Identity itself is built on the will of power and defines itself in the negative, on the capacity of destruction and abuse of the other.[15]

While in *The Place*, meeting the dark side of God and of the individual can generate hatred towards oneself as a human being, still stuck at the abuse of the weak, at the *libido dominandi*, at the violence against the neighbour, the animals, and nature, still stuck at rapacity, at selfishness, at barbarism, despite millennia of evolution of the Soul.

The exceptional creative capacities of human beings, visible in all the multiple forms of art or in knowledge, cannot balance their miserable primary nature, being, exactly, an exception.[16]

For the sake of personal, national, cultural, religious identity, an unjustifiable quantity of suffering has been (and still is) inflicted on numberless individuals.

It's hard to acknowledge any meaning in what one sees from the perspective of *The Place*. The future advent of God's truth, the fight between Good and Evil, creation that comes from destruction, the necessity of pain in order to individuate and grow, the self-unfolding of the Soul, everything sounds like "bullshit", while in *The Place*.

As a metaphysically naked analyst myself, I could not state any of these pre-modern explanations, while witnessing once again Job's desperation in the post-modern era.

Amanda Wilhelmina would hardly accept any of them, were she looking into my eyes today.

The quest for meaning after the end of meaning

If the end of in-ness is the logical passage to a new collective form of being-in-the-world of the Western consciousness, I suggest it is a *Job Experience*, on the individual level, the passage bringing to conscious awareness being born out of the in-ness.

After this passage, the metaphysically naked man really faces the unprecedented problem of finding some meaning after the end of the previous frames of meaning. This problem is faced experiencially, while in *The Place*, and not from a mere philosophical point of view, that is a much safer perspective.

The stage of metaphysical teenage could be the starting point of a process of revision of the traditional image of God, in first place.

In order to orientate oneself in the complex issue of Evil, one could benefit from Paul Ricoeur's work,[17] while Hans Jonas' contribution could be useful for revising the traditional image of God.[18] Yet, both these authors have the limit that they write within the in-ness, so to say. Although acknowledging that Evil can only come from God, for instance, Ricoeur states we have to believe in God *despite* Evil; while Jonas, in order to keep the criteria of God's omnibenevolence and comprehensibility, sacrifices His omnipotence. Neither of the two gives up the in-ness.

Nevertheless, Jonas' speculation about God who gives up His transcendence, throwing Himself in temporality, in order to be present in the creation, to start it, can be interesting for our purpose.

God descends in Space and Time and is changed in His own essence by this descent.

Jonas refers to some ideas expressed in the Lurianic Kabbalah,[19] returning to us the image of an eternal entity who becomes immanent, immersed in temporality.

In the light of these references, one could no more think of God as an antropomorphous being, existing somewhere *out there*, in opposition to where we exist, *here*. God cannot be seen any more as a good father as well, but only as an eternal *primum movens* who "plays temporal", so to say.

This perspective might imply the divinity of every single particle of the universe. Every existing thing, including us, could be seen as a fragment of the Being thrown into temporality.

Yet, while in *The Place*, one is hardly consoled by this view, because it does not offer any special frame of meaning to the suffering of the metaphysically naked man. On another hand, the typical consequences of questioning the traditional image of God, namely atheism ("there is no God", no *primum movens*) and nihilism ("nothing has meaning"), appear to be completely senseless.

First of all, they apparently deny the evidence that we are thrown into a pre-existing material world brutally imposing on us, and turning us, willy-nilly, in suffering subjects (*sub*-jectum, thrown under, "subject to"). Second, if nothing has meaning and there is no *principium*, there would be no moral restraint to Evil, no reason to avoid doing it. The consequent authorisation to do the evil, that is, the most common and present thing in the creation, would precisely correspond to a complete philosophical and existential failure.

The profound rage against the injustice of the whole of creation that one feels in *The Place* would require a total revolt against everything, human and divine, creation and creator, God and Devil, an attempt to go beyond human and divine, so to say. The first and most rebellious action would be to try do good, namely the rarest event in our entropic universe.

This kind of rebellion against the basic element of our structure (primary narcissism, will of power, possession, the tyranny of the Ego, the destructive defence of egoic identity), as well as the revolt against the previous frames of meaning and the old positive image of God would be part of the process of going "out of the egg of in-ness".

After questioning the traditional image of God, we said, man becomes aware of his metaphysical nakedness, and finally enters a stage of adulthood. Now the individual has moved out of his parents' house, and finds himself standing on his own feet. But is this kind of adulthood really possible to stand?

What Jung did, in Giegerich's opinion, that is, to re-establish a sort of in-ness, is apparently what comes naturally to our psyche, in most cases. Jung's quotation of Tertullian that the Soul is naturally religious appears here in its ultimate truth. Often autonomously and unconsciously, the psyche restores some sort of frame or container, as if this were its typical way of functioning.

The production of symbols apparently aims towards this goal, and being an analyst, I would never interfere with such a process in a patient, rather I would facilitate it and encourage it.

From this perspective, Jung may have not invented the unconscious for the personal purpose of restoring a symbolic life, as Giegerich claims, but because the symbolic life is the natural activity of the Soul, it restored itself in that magmatic form Jung had somehow to shape.

Actually, I would not exclude the possibility of multiple, simultaneous activities of the Soul, like setting a new logic form of being-in-the-world (out of the in-ness), on one hand, and behaving still as a *"symbolic in-ness- builder"* on the other.

Definitely, the issue of the end of in-ness, together with the unresolved problem of Evil, appear to be the fundamental questions of the postmodern world, the invisible water we are all swimming in, suddenly and painfully visible when one is thrown into what we have called *The Place*.

A psychology aimed only at restoring the individual's functioning, and at reaching a form of presupposed well-being, definitely seems an *opus parvum*, a laughable way to ignore and deny these fundamental issues.

On the other hand, if psychology is a self-expression of the psyche creating and investigating itself, being in *The Place*, such a psychology seems a trick to avoid the evidence of being at the same time a living/dying body in the material world, subject-ed to life.

We inhabit *Midgard*, being fragile bodies, exposed on the surface of an isolated planet, at the outskirts of the universe, leaning onto a mystery.

The quest for meaning after the end of meaning is a fully psychological issue, a painful issue when it comes to a wounded Ego facing the presence of Evil in the material world. The experience of radical Evil can again and suddenly transform us into "Job". Yet, a third-millennium Job would neither find any God in front of him, nor some easy container.

The individual who has taken note of the end of in-ness would try to inhabit this new logic form of being-in-the-world actively, without restoring a sort of psychological childhood, but still necessarily looking for some meaning (in German *sinn*, which also implies direction). It is definitely a difficult position.

As though to mock my efforts in getting to a conclusion of these pages, a dream came while I was writing.

I saw a friend of my wife, a person who had successfully recovered from a painful past of drug and alcohol abuse, giving birth to a child. The child was then going to be mine and my wife's. While the nurses were carrying the child in a blanket, I saw him, amidst shit and blood.

He was shitting as well, while his face was nice, and smiling to me.

I welcomed him into this world, giving a fillip on his little nose, smiling back to him.

The psyche keeps speaking from the darkness, and we keep facing its mystery, in this new era as well.

Instead of focusing on the symbol of a divine child, could it be that this dream shows that I should meet and welcome the soul, the Self, or the psyche as an adult?

Suggestions

Dostoyevski, F. (2003). *The Brothers Karamazov*. London: Penguin Books.
Dürrenmatt, F. (2011). *Der Tunnel*. Zürich: Diogenes Verlag.
Galimberti, U. (2001). *La terra senza il male. Jung: dall'inconscio al simbolo*. Milan: Feltrinelli.
Galimberti, U. (2002). *Psiche e techne. L'uomo nell'età della tecnica*. Milan: Feltrinelli.
Jonas, H. (1987). *Der Gottesbegriff nach Auschwitz. Eine judische Stimme*. Berlin: Suhrkamp Verlag.
Leopardi, G. (1982). *Operette morali*. Milan: Ugo Mursia editore.
Levi, P. (1991). *If This Is a Man—The Truce*. London: Abacus Books.
Levi, P. (1989). *The Drowned and the Saved*. London: Abacus Books.
Ricoeur, P. (1986). *Le mal. Un défi á la philosophie et á la théologie*. Genéve: Labor et Fides.
Riel, J. (1975). *Før morgendagen*. København: Lademann.
Shalamov, V. (1995). *Kolyma Tales*. London: Penguin Books.
Tillich, P. (1952). *The Courage to Be*. New Haven: Yale University Press.
Wiesel, E. (2008). *Night*. London: Penguin Books.

BM

1. See Giegerich, W., *Das Ende des Sinns und die Geburt des Menschen* (English translation: *The End of Meaning and the Birth of Man*, at the link http://www.cgjungpage.org/pdfdocuments/EndofMeaning.pdf).
2. Ibid., p. 15.
3. Ibid., p. 14.
4. Jung, C. G., *Letters 2*, p. 586, to Berann, 27 August 1960.
5. Heidegger M., *Nietzsche*, (1936–1946, 1961); translation in Italian *Nietzsche*, Milan: Adelphi, 1994.
6. Severino reckons that Greek philosophy has set the meaning of "becoming" as "coming out of nothing and returning again to nothing". The "faith in becoming", the trust that Being oscillates between a previous nothing (*nihil*, in Latin) and a following nothing, is considered by Severino as the premise to any form of will of power and the real essence of nihilism.
7. For a deeper review of this issue, see the chapter entitled *Closing Chords: Possibility and Limit*, in my book *The Labyrinth of Possibility: A Therapeutic Factor in Analytical Practice*. London: Karnac Books, 2014.
8. Giegerich, W., *Das Ende des Sinns und die Geburt des Menschen*, p. 9.
9. See in this regard Anders, G. (1980). *Die Antiquiertheit des Menschen, Band I: Über die Seele im Zeitalter der zweiten industriellen Revolution*. München: Verlag C. H. Bech; Anders, G. (1995). *Die Antiquiertheit des Menschen,*

Band II: Über die Zerstörung des Lebens im Zeitalter der dritten industriellen Revolution. München: Verlag C. H. Bech; Galimberti, U. (2002). *Psiche e techne*. Milano: Feltrinelli.

10. "The condition of the possibility of the sacred, the numinous, of mysteries, of the symbolic life, of myth and religion—each taken according to its highest determination—has disappeared" (Giegerich, W., *Das Ende des Sinns und die Geburt des Menschen*, pp. 18–22).
11. "How can consciousness, once it has been born out of the in-ness in meaning and its *irreversible* bornness has been fully realized, become unborn again?" (Giegerich, W., *Das Ende des Sinns und die Geburt des Menschen*, p. 33).
12. "And if the sufferings of children go to swell the sum of sufferings which was necessary to pay for truth, then I protest that the truth is not worth such a price"; Dostoevski, F., *The Brothers Karamazov*, part II, book V, Chapter Four: Rebellion.
13. Personal communication.
14. The profound rage that dominates the stage of metaphysical teenage must be clearly distinguished from the destructive rage often characterising the real teenage or the borderline personality. While in the metaphysical teenage, one hates exactly the borderline destructiveness, toward the others or towards oneself, because it is seen as the sign of the essential failure of the whole creation project.
15. "The subject says to the object: 'I have destroyed you', and the object is there to receive the communication. From now on the subject says, 'Hullo, object! I've destroyed you.' 'I love you.' 'You have value for me because of your survival of my destruction of you.' 'While I am loving you, I am all the time destroying you in (unconscious) fantasy'" (Winnicott, D. W. (2005). *The Use of an Object and Relating through Identifications*. In *Playing and Reality*. London: Routledge). Certainly very precious for a deeper understanding of psychic functioning and of building of the Ego, this description by Winnicott, from the point of view of *The Place*, brings us to the conclusion that the human being, in his essence, basically sucks.
16. Notwithstanding, art, like dreams and creative activities, offers some hope for the possibility of transcending the miserable ingredients on which human being's structure is based.
17. Ricoeur, P. (1986).
18. Jonas, H. (1987).
19. See Jonas' reference to the doctrine of Tzimtzum, according to which God began the process of creation by contracting his infinite light to allow a finite space were Becoming could start.

INDEX

a world clothed in nudity, 17
Aalsmeer, 19
actions, 20–21
Adamo, Pietro, 30, 84 n13
addiction, 6, 17
Adonis, 63
advertising, 14–16, 26
Akkadians, 65
amateur porn, 28, 30
Anahita, 70
anasyrma, 64–65
Anath, 70
Anders, Günther, 3–9, 14–17
   a world clothed in nudity, 17
   advertising, 14–16
   Coca-Cola, 5
   "I was only doing my duty", 20
   "iconomania", 7
   reversal of perspective, 3
   system of apparatuses, 4, 6
   "The obsolescence of privacy", 8
   "The obsolescence of the individual", 14–15
   third industrial revolution, 4
   voyeurs, 9
Anderson, Rafaela, 87 n11
anima, 97
"Answer to Job" (C. G. Jung), 100
anti-porn activists, 32, 41, 74
anxiety, 83 n7
Aphrodite, 62–66, 70, 77
archetypes, 35, 62, 98
Arendt, Hannah, 21
Aristotle, 61
arousal, 53–56
Ashtart, 70
Ashtoreth, 65
Astarte, 65, 70
attention, 15
autonomous complexes, 76

Babylonia, 70
Bataille, Georges, 56, 80 n2 (Chapter Two)
Bauman, Zygmunt, 27
body, the, 47–49
    advertising and the female body, 16
    decision making about, 28
    disconnection from, 49
    playing and, 47–48
    porn and, 55
    rejoicing in, 39–40, 43
    repression of, 38, 61
    word derivations, xi
Brothers Karamazov, The (Fyodor Dostoevski), 100–101
Buddha, 67

Canaanites, 70
capitalism, 14, 18, 24, 37–38
children, 14, 42, 47
Chomsky, Noam, 11
Christianity, 35, 37, 61, 71
Chronos, 62
cinema, 1
Coca-Cola, 5
collaborators, 23–24
collective unconscious, the, 34, 98
commandments, 11
commodities, 9, 15
complexity, ix–x
connectedness, 5
consciousness
    being in the world, 102
    collective, 50
    difference and, 60
    history of, x, 16, 25, 61, 66, 71, 74, 95–98
    shadow and, 33
consumption, 8–11
    destruction of environment and, 43
    mandatory consumers, 22–23
    porn and, 48, 73
    production of needs and, 4–5
    voyeurism and, 50
courting, 17
creation (original), 101–102
creativity, 47–48
customer dissatisfaction, 11
Cybele, 70

Danish Code of Laws, xi
death, 82 n3
Deep Throat (Gerard Damiano), xi, 29
degradation, 56–57, 86 n5
Demeter, 64
Denmark, 2, 29
dependency, 6
Derrida, Jacques, 86 n5
desire, 36–39, 51
destructiveness, 39–43, 84 n11, 107 n15
differentiation *see* non-differentiation
Dionysus, 63–64
disenchantment, 97
displacement, 57–58, 60, 68–69
dissociation, 43, 75–77
Di(zion)ario erotico (Massimo Fini), 56
doing, 20–21
domination, 47, 50
Dostoevski, Fyodor, 100–101
drug addiction, 72–73
duty, 20
DVDs, 2–3

ego
    development through play and creativity, 47
    dialogue with the unconscious, 35
    ego complex, 27
    ego-personality, 34

INDEX

facing Evil, 105
keeping control, 37
language and, 84 n9
narcissism and, 39, 102
tyranny of, 104
Winnicott and, 107 n15
Egypt (Ancient), 61, 70
Eichmann, Adolf, 21
Eliade, Mircea
   desacralisation, 97
   Hinduism, 67
   initiation, disappearance of, 72
   manifestation of the sacred, 61
   non-religious people's continuing behaviour patterns, 71
emancipation (of women), 28–30, 38
Enlightenment, the 95, 97
Eros, 62
eros, 35
eroticism, 63, 88 n20
Evil, 35, 99–105
extermination camps, 19–21
extra-marital sex, 38
eyes, 10

facial expression, 29, 58–59
father principle, 16, 26
Fini, Massimo, 56
Finland, 19, 53–54, 81 n3
FINSEX, 53
France, 29
free web platforms, 23
Freud, Sigmund, 33
fucking machine, 89 n5
Furies, the, 65

gang bang, 81 n5
genitals, 59, 86 n3, 87 n11
Giegerich, Wolfgang, 96, 98, 101, 104
Ginestra, La (Giacomo Leopardi), 100
Girard, René, 34
Gnosticism, 61

God, 96, 98, 100–105
Greeks (Classical)
   Aphrodite, 64, 70
   gods as archetypes, 62
   Mediterranean cults, 61
   prostitutes in, xi, 75
   symbol and porn derivations, x–xi
growth (economic), 26

Hantzis, Marina Ann, 88–89 n3
Hartley, Nina, 89–90 n12
Hathor, 70
Hebrews, 65
Heidegger, Martin, 25, 96
Helsinki, 12, 19, 81 n3, 99
Hera, 62
Heraclitus, 88 n13
Herman, Edward S., 11
Hermes, 63
Herrenabende, 79 n2 (Chapter One)
Hesiod, 64
Hietaniemi, 99
Hillman, James, 62–63, 65
Hinduism, 61, 67
Holland, 19, 21, 80 n1 (Chapter Four)
hotels, 35
"How To Disappear Completely" (Radiohead), 90 n13

"I was only doing my duty", 20
iconomania, 7
identity, sense of, 27
images, 6–12, 42–43, 49, 58
imagination, 47, 62
Inanna, 65, 70
individuals, 27, 101
individuation, 34, 37, 42, 73
Industrial Revolution, 24–25, 95, 97
   second, 4
   third, 4
initiation, 72–73

internet
  children access, 14
  impact on porn market, 30
  porn on, x, 11, 53
  research of use of, 36
inurement, 42–43
Ishtar, 65, 70
Isis, 70

Jameson, Jenna, 86 n7
Job, Book of, 99–101, 105
Jonas, Hans, 103
jouissance, 55
Judaism, 35, 61, 71
Jung, C. G.
  "Answer to Job", 100
  autonomous complexes, 76
  creative activity of imagination, 47
  ego complex, the, 27
  individuation, 42, 73
  interpretation, 63
  lack of meaning in modernity, 97
  loneliness without limit, 96
  male and female within all, 68
  porn as symbol, x
  religion and sexuality, 61
  Self, 98
  shadow, the, 33–35

Kabbalah, Lurianic, 103
Kenya, 19, 21, 24, 80 n1 (Chapter Four)
Kerényi, Károly, 65
Klein, Melanie, 55

Lacan, Jacques, xii, 55
Leopardi, Giacomo, 96
lesbianism, 69
Levinas, Emmanuel, 68
limits, 25–32, 73, 97, 100
liquid identities, 27–28
logos, 35

Love on the Road (exhibition), 89 n12
Lovelace, Linda, 29, 82 n7
Lurianic Kabbalah, 103

machines, 4 *see also* technology
markets, 17
masturbation, 36, 39
Max Hardcore, 84 n13
meaning, 96–98, 103–105
Mediterranean, the, 61
mediums, 49
men in porn, 31, 40–41, 46, 59
men watching porn, 36, 46, 74–75, 83 n5
Mesopotamia, 61, 65
metaphysical nakedness, 71
metaphysical teenagers, 101, 103, 107 n14 *see also* teenagers
Midgard, 95, 100, 105
Moore, Thomas, 65, 86 n2
morality, public, 16
multiplicity (of desire), 37–38
music, 18, 49
myth, 63

nakedness, metaphysical, 71
narcissism, 36, 38–39, 54, 102
narrative elements, 45–46
Nazism, 19–21
need, 4–5, 37
Netherlands, 19, 21
Neumann, Erich, 42
Nietzsche, Friedrich, 25, 96
non-differentiation, 57–61, 74–76
  Aphrodite, ancient ritual and, 66
  Sasha Gray, 89 n3
  women and men polarities, 68–69, 88 n2
numinosity, 61, 65–66, 74–77

"obsolescence of privacy, The" (Günther Anders), 8

"obsolescence of the individual, The", (Günther Anders), 14–15
Oedipus, 55–56
offers, 11
omnipotence, 26
Otto, Rudolf, 61

patriarchal values
    advent of, 71
    fading of, 16, 28–29
    logos and *eros*, 35
    male scholars and, 44
    repression and, 39
    sex outside marriage and, 38
Paul, Pamela, 13–14, 17
Pauli, Wolfgang, 97
pay-per-view TV, 3
Persephone, 64
phantoms, 7–12, 49–50
photography, 1
Pink Madness (James Hillman), 62
play, 47–48
politicians, 16
"porn portions", 45, 48
Pornified: How Pornography Is Damaging Our Lives, Our Relationships, and Our Families (Pamela Paul), 13
pornography (and porn), xi–xii
pornscapes, 9, 58
pre-views, 10–11
Priapus, 62–63
production, 4–5, 14–18, 26
professional porn movies, 29
projection, 33
prostitutes, x–xi, 28, 70–71, 75
psyche, the
    complexity of, x
    individuation and, 42
    Jung on, 34, 61
    masculine and feminine, 40, 68
psychoanalysis, 39, 55, 63, 102
publicity, 16

Qualls-Corbett, Nancy, xiii, 70

Radiohead, 90 n13
rage, 101, 107 n14
Regazzoni, S., 59, 86 n5
religion
    behaviour and, 71
    sexuality and, 35, 37, 61, 65–66, 70
repression, 25–27, 37–39
reversal of perspective, 3
Ricoeur, Paul, 103
rites of passage, 72
ritual, 63, 72–73
Rome (Classical), 61, 64
roses, 19, 21–22

Sacred, The (Rudolf Otto), 61
Saturn productions, 79 n2 (Chapter One)
Schiller, Friedrich, 47
Schwarz, Annette, 82 n9, 89 n11
second industrial revolution, 4
Second World War, 19–21
seduction, 15–18
self-knowledge, 34
Severino, Emanuele, 96, 106 n6
sexuality, 47–50
    death and, 82 n3
    degradation of women, and, 56
    porn and, x
    religion and, 35, 37, 61, 65–66, 70
    separation from reproductive function, 28–31, 38
shadow, the, 33–44, 56, 65, 77–78
Siffredi, Rocco, 84 n13
sirens, 11, 17
smartphones, 49
social media, 18, 49

Song of Songs (Old Testament), 88 n15
Soul, the, 102, 104
spectators *see* voyeurs
Suhonen, Paola, 89–90 n12
Sumer, 65
symbols, xii, 104
system of apparatuses, 4–6

taboo, 36
Tara, 67
technology, 1–6
    capitalism and, 14
    omnipotent domination of, 25, 97
    shadow of, 77
teenagers, 14, 42 *see also*
    metaphysical teenagers
TePaske, Bradley, 35, 83 n6
Tertullian, 104
third industrial revolution, 4, 14
Time magazine, 13–14
transgression, 31, 60
types of porn, 54
Tzimtzum, 107 n19

unconscious, the, 33–35
United States
    hard-core movies in, 2, 29
    political marketing in, 16
    porn infiltrates, 14
    roses from Aalsmeer, 19

Vasistha, 67
VCR (Video Cassette Recording), 2
Venus, 70, 77 *see also* Aphrodite
VHS, 2
visibility, 27–28
vision, 10, 49
voyeurs, 8–11
    access for, 23–24, 58
    docility of, 50
    landscape of porn and, 17
    role of, 46
    senses utilised by, 48

Weber, Max, 97
Weil, Simone, 101
Wilhelmina, Amanda, 98–99, 102
Winnicott, Donald W., 47, 84 n11, 107 n15
women in porn, 57–60
    absence of pleasure in, 46
    Aphrodite and, 63–65
    denial of limits, 31–32
    entering the realm of the sacred, 68
    lack of awareness of numinosity, 74–77
    stripped bare, 40–41
women watching porn, 44, 53–54
women's emancipation, 28–30, 38
working, 20–21
World Wide Web, 2, 23

Yow, Bobbie, 62–63, 65

Zeus, 62–63
Zoja, Luigi, 72–73
Zyklon B, 20